The Younger Mouse Gets the Cheese:

A Youth's Guide to Investment

by
Patrick Pappano

www.theyoungermouse.com

ISBN 978-0-9889127-1-7
Library of Congress Control Number: 2014914270

This book is dedicated to my uncle Kevin Corrigan, who introduced me to the idea of investing in the stock market when I was in high school and urged me to open an account at Merrill Lynch.

Edited by Gretchen Wagner
Proofread by Laura M. Reden

Also by Patrick Pappano:
Owning Main Street: A Beginner's Guide to the Stock Market
www.owningmainstreet.com
Cardyf Publishing, 2013

Published by:
Cardyf Publishing
632B Heritage Village
Southbury CT 06488
(203) 405-3433

AMSTERDAM — Greenpeace International has acknowledged losing 3.8 million euros ($5.2 million) on a bet the euro would not strengthen against other currencies in 2013— but it did.

The environmental group, which is based in Amsterdam, said the money was lost by an employee who acted beyond the limits of his authority but had hoped to benefit the organization.

Greenpeace did not identify the employee, who has been fired, and added there was no evidence of fraud.

In a statement Monday, Greenpeace apologized for the blunder to supporters and donors and said it was studying what went wrong.

It said it would absorb the loss over a period of several years by trimming "infrastructure investments."

The group pledged not to reduce spending on campaigns to protect the environment.

New York Times, Monday June 16, 2014

Contents

Foreword

ONE EVOLUTION ALL PEOPLE UNDERGO, from infancy to old age, is the cost of their maintenance. Babies are relatively easy to maintain, being satisfied with the basics plus a few toys like rattles and blocks. But as we grow older, our surroundings become more critical. Clothes become more important and we are no longer satisfied with rattles and blocks but demand televisions and bicycles and more. Most of these things aren't necessities in the strict sense of the word but are desired to allow us to continue on a path of self-discovery, engaging our surroundings and engaging other people. We have to have the right clothes and the right toys to present ourselves to others as we wish to be understood. Then we will graduate from high school and life will change. Some of us will go to college and others will go into the military or to work. Regardless of the path taken, what comes into focus is the sudden emergence of the need for self-reliance. It is you who will pay the bills now and your parents are no longer there for every bruise. Life starts coming at you in real-time.

It is at this point in our lives that we incur the envy of our elders, who will frequently be heard saying: *"If only I could start over,"* or *"How lucky you are to be in your youth."* We greet such pronouncements with bewilderment – what are they talking about?

They are speaking of the divide between carefree youth and care-burdened adulthood. As we continue on our path of aging, the natural growth of things we have to have will crowd out those things we would like to have. Soon there are very few toys, and responsibilities take up our entire lives. The bloom of youth is gone - we are now adults with grownup problems and often not enough resources to solve all those problems. That is where the care comes in, and we will find ourselves hugging nieces and nephews and telling them how lucky they are to have their youth so they can do a better job of working out their future.

How we meet our growing obligations will be decided pretty much by personal habits we put into place in our youth. So right now is the time, as Paul of Tarsus said, to put away childish things. But don't be dismayed, a little thinking and planning now will go a long way to providing you with a life that may very well have a few toys in it and not be so burdened with care. You see, what youth has that your elders are so envious of, is time. Just time alone will do a lot of your work for you if you plan. The envious elders did not plan and want to start over with greater wisdom and foresight. But we all know time only passes us by once, there are no second chances. This book is about helping you build up your resources so that as life comes at you, you will be as ready as you need to be.

Chapter 1

Income & Expenses

IF YOU ARE LIKE MOST PEOPLE, some day you will have to go to work and earn a living to pay for the necessities of life: food, shelter, clothing, a car, and any number of additional items you need on a day-to-day basis just to function in your world. And if you are like most people, in the beginning you will probably not earn enough to take care of all of your needs. That point may not be reached until you reach age 40 or later. After that you will be on the other side of your life, when you will earn more than you need but will have to plan for a day when earnings stop but life goes on – retirement. So learning to manage now for looming mountains of need later is the hallmark of good planning and wisdom.

There are many dimensions to the planning we must do for life, like eating healthy now for a time in our future when our bodies slow down and can't metabolize a youthful diet of cheeseburgers, fries and milkshakes. Taking care of our teeth in our youth will pay big dividends later on. But the dimension of planning this book is concerned with is savings – starting a savings program to help you meet financial needs in the future. Since time is on your side you can act now and let time do most of the work.

What do we mean by time doing most of the work for our savings? Well, let's say you decided to save $10 a month and put it into a passbook savings account at a bank that pays 5% interest. That means that every year the bank adds 5% to your money so that after 1 year the first $10 is now worth $10.50. After the second year, $10.50 grows to $11.02. After ten years, the original $10 grows to $16.28, all without any effort on your part. This is the wonderful part about savings, that not only does the money you deposited grow, but the money it earns grows too. This is called *compound interest*; it is a money growing machine and all you have to do is....nothing!

Just to illustrate, say you did put away $10 per month in a passbook savings account at 5% interest, what would the accumulation be after 50 years? $26,492. If instead you put the money to work in the stock market, what would the accumulation be after 50 years? $154,809 at a 10% annualized return. For $10 per month, that is a breathtaking result and a demonstration of the magic of compound return and time.

Your First Job

When you go to work on your first job, you may, like the author, be excited at the size of your first paycheck. But that paycheck will soon shrink as you go about paying for those things you need, like shelter, food and clothing and a car. Just those things will eat up most of your paycheck. After a while, it will seem like you are just living to work. Well, there is a lot of truth to that, and what you will find is that you must, perhaps for the first time, plan your life very carefully. As you grow older and more experienced, you will earn more, but it won't seem that way because expenses always expand to meet wages. That promotion at work will prompt you to need better clothes and a better car, perhaps. Whatever the cause, that state where income vastly outweighs expenses is far into the future and for many may never come at all. The lesson here is very important: expenses are slippery and it will take a great deal of discipline to drive them down to a point where you see daylight – daylight being that fraction where income exceeds expenses. It is very hard work but crucial to managing your financial life.

In the balancing act of stretching income to match or exceed expenses there is a rule that is passed down from generation to generation: *"Pay yourself first."* Yes, you must be your first creditor. You should give yourself 5% of every paycheck and put it into savings and forget it. There will always be very compelling reasons to raid your savings but they must be resisted or you will have no savings.

The Role of Knowledge

The reason you are paid so little when you start out is that although you may be educated, education is just a tool. Until you put that tool to work and create value, you just aren't worth that much. But as you gain experience, your ability to create value will grow and you will be paid a growing wage for it. That means that every day and week and month and year that you are on your job you gain knowledge that makes you better at your job, and your work becomes more valuable. As your work becomes more valuable, your wages rise. But here is a crucial point. That added knowledge you are accumulating cannot be taken away from you, it is yours alone and it is part of who you are. With time, your work has greater value and commands higher wages. Now, let's say some emergency came up and somebody offered you money for some of your knowledge. You have an emergency; the way to meet that emergency is to give up some of your knowledge; then the emergency passes. But you will then have to go back to a smaller wage and it may take several years to get back to where you were; by that time, your co-workers would have surged ahead with their accumulated knowledge. You will find yourself forever behind.

Fortunately that will never happen – no one can take your knowledge from you, and your knowledge then forms your most reliable resource. Your growing workplace knowledge will determine not only your income but many other dimensions of your life, like job satisfaction and overall life satisfaction. Many people may never take stock of the role their occupational knowledge plays in their life, but it pretty much determines the quality of the life they live.

Life savings are like occupational knowledge in that those savings will play a big part in determining the quality of life you lead, but there is one huge difference —nobody can rob you of your knowledge but "emergencies" can rob you of your savings.

Emergencies look very different depending on whether you can afford them or not. For people who can afford their emergencies, they are an inconvenience. Emergencies that cannot be afforded become a crisis and often a life-changing event. So another rule on life is that emergencies will happen. The best thing to do is first of all, avoid them, and then plan for the ones that can't be avoided. And of course, there is the biggest dimension of all – is it really an emergency? A savings program often succeeds because savings are given higher priority than "emergencies." In judging whether an event rises to the level of an emergency that justifies raiding savings, remember: too many emergencies and you won't have savings. Better to reserve savings for real emergencies.

Lifestyle Choices

This is not a book about lifestyle choices, but there are choices in life that carry differing risk profiles; higher-risk lifestyles will inevitably produce more emergencies. Choosing lower-risk will, in the long run, reduce the incidence of emergencies and give you greater control over your life.

One choice you will be required to make is diet. It has been postulated that over 5 million years our species, *Homo sapiens sapiens*, led a very dangerous life that required a very high nutritional diet to survive. That arduous lifestyle has given way to a largely sedentary way of life but only in the past few thousand years; the high demand diet imprinted on our DNA over millions of years still determines our choices even while our physical exertions are low. We still eat as if we lived in the jungle and hunted for our food while trying not to become food ourselves. That took a lot of work. All that work at one time pretty much worked off the diet, but no more. That residual dietary programming shows up as un-worked-off fat that will inevitably lead to health problems. Choosing a low-fat diet is only one lifestyle choice that you will be confronted with that over time will make a dramatic difference on the quality of life you live. Like accumulating occupational knowledge and accumulating savings, lifestyle choices also accumulate and have results of their own. It is much easier to make the right choice right at the start because once made, basic choices are hard, if not almost impossible, to turn around. In life, all brooks eventually turn into rivers. Be sure you are on the right side of the brook when you start out – rivers are difficult to cross.

Why this detour into lifestyle, isn't this a book about investment? Investment is rooted in lifestyle. As soon as an investment program is decided upon, choices will have to be made. And just as it is easier to just continue lifestyle choices that seem popular and comfortable, investment choices that seem popular and therefore comfortable will be the easiest to select. But it must be presented at the outset: "popular" and "comfortable" don't work in investment. Investment is about doing the right thing with sometimes nothing more to go on than instinct. Often investment is counter-intuitive, or doing nothing when a situation screams out for action. Investment comes from within, and successful investment comes from a within that has been carefully constructed. The first mouse just wants the cheese; the second mouse thinks before acting.

The Speed of Life

This is a book about investment, intended to help you accumulate enough wealth to finance aspirations in life that are a long way off and are not visible today. Those aspirations will be needs some day, but only at a point in your life when it is too late to

Be doing anything about them. That is the way life works, unfortunately; the need only shows up well after the point you could have prepared for that need. To give you a sense of that phenomenon in life, just ask a few older people you encounter what they would have done differently in their lives if given the opportunity to start over. Be prepared for an outpouring of missed opportunities, wrong choices and shortsighted decisions.

What you will hear is that essentially life came at people at a speed they were unaware of and unprepared for. For younger people, life seems to be moving at a snail's pace, but that is just poor vision; life is actually coming at you very rapidly and you just can't see it. What you will learn, however, is that the choices you make will be the result of the totality of the individual that is you, constructed from all those choices you made every day of your life.

Choices are directions whose implications may not be known for some time. It is only after graduating from high school that those differences will come into view. Friends you thought you knew will head off in different directions you won't understand. You will get together with them sometime after graduation, and instead of the intimate camaraderie of past years there will be awkward silences as you realize that you are different people on different journeys. You will think back to points in time when you might have detected the differences you see now, and you will wonder where the compatibility came from. It came from the fact that you were all making choices, but those choices would not manifest themselves for some time – that time is now.

The way you manage income and expenses will be the result of lifestyle choices you make. Some will make those choices based on what they see at that instant. More thoughtful people may put off making some choices until they have more information. But there will always be information you don't have, that you can only guess at. Thinking that there might be more to life than what you see at the present instant, and wishing to make some provision for that unknown, to prepare you for the future, is the beginning of a wisdom that, taken to its logical conclusion, will create for you a significantly better lifetime experience chock-full of better decisions leading to better outcomes. It all starts with recognition that there is a future – you just can't see it yet.

How Money is Treated in a Household

Between my freshman and sophomore years at college I had a summer job as a Fuller Brush salesman, a job no longer available in modern society or the United States of the 21st century.

I would distribute 12-page catalogs to households in a neighborhood every evening then go around door-to-door the following day, hoping housewives had studied the catalogs and had orders ready for me to fill.

I soon learned that sales didn't just happen, and that my job was to inspire these women to order merchandise. But then another problem arose: when I would make deliveries on Saturdays, the husband was home and would refuse the delivery, and I was out not only the sale but also the cost of the order.

My boss told me to always collect a deposit so the husband would have to either pay or give up the deposit. In such cases, the husbands mostly paid. But there was a problem with taking deposits too. Deposits often got raided to pay for staples like food during the week, so when the Fuller Brush bill arrived there wasn't enough money to pay the bill and you didn't get product to fulfill orders you had already sold.

At a sales meeting I attended, one of the speakers described leaving the business because he could never pay the Fuller Brush bill – the deposit money had been spent on other things. After failing to make a good wage at his new job, he returned to Fuller Brush and described his new process for handling deposits. He would put all deposits into a safe that only he knew the combination to. No matter what household need came up, the safe could not be opened except when it came time to pay the Fuller Brush bill, and that got paid first. With this security process in place, he described not only being able to work productively, but for the first time, he and his wife had savings. The discipline had changed the way they managed all the dimensions of their lives and gave them a sense of control they hadn't experienced before – control led to savings.

So savings can be what is left over after the "necessities" have been paid, in which case there will be no savings; or savings can be first, where you pay yourself first and whatever gets paid after that is a "necessity" only because it gets paid for.

Chapter 2

Savings

WHY DOES THE BANK PAY INTEREST? After all, if the bank is holding your money for safekeeping so that it will always be there when you want it, and the bank is accounting for it, shouldn't you be paying them for their service? One would think so, but the bank actually does not house your money for safekeeping, they put your money to work and so pay you to use your money.

Banks are in the business of taking in deposits and using those deposits to make loans. If they pay depositors 5% and charge lenders 10%, they keep 5% as income from which they deduct the expense of taking in and doling out money to arrive at their profit.

Most banks have what is called a *portfolio* of loans which spreads their risk so if they fail to collect on one or more loans they aren't out of business. The loan failure is just added to their expenses and may prompt them to reduce interest paid on deposits and increase interest on loans or increase their spread. If the spread gets too wide, they will begin to lose business to more efficient banks and will then have to become more efficient themselves to stay in business.

Origin of Banks

Back in the days before money, gold was often the means of exchange because it was in general supply, highly valued by all and easily divisible into different-sized pieces. But the value of gold brought with it vulnerability to theft, so holders of gold used to deposit the gold with goldsmiths who knew how to safely secure gold. Depositors of gold would then be given a receipt as proof of ownership.

At first when purchases were made, a trip to the goldsmith was required to retrieve the necessary quantity of gold to conclude the transaction, but after a while, holders of gold used to just give up their receipts in exchange for whatever it was they wanted. The gold receipts became the first paper money.

The goldsmiths noticed that while the gold changed ownership, it was almost never retrieved from their vaults, so they conceived of the idea of making loans with that gold, feeling sure the loans would be repaid before claims for the gold were made. This worked out and soon goldsmiths were sources for loans. Eventually, since loans generated revenue, it was only natural that gold depositors should demand fees for use of their gold, so you have what today has become interest on deposits and interest on loans. Banks, the modern version of yesterday's goldsmiths, then take the spread between what they have to pay for deposits and what they can charge for loans.

Banks are central to commercial life, and to encourage savings have their deposits guaranteed by the federal government. At the start of The Great Depression of 1929, all the depositors panicked and demanded their money back, fearing the banks might not be able to collect their loans. Since the money was out on loan the banks didn't have enough ready cash to pay depositors and the banks closed as a result of not meeting depositors' demand for their funds. To prevent that from happening again, the federal government guarantees deposits through the FDIC (Federal Deposit Insurance Corporation). Since establishment of the FDIC, there have not been any bank runs.

Mortgages

Taking in deposits is the easy part; the hard part of banking is figuring out what to do with the money. This quandary is resolved for most banks by making real estate loans called mortgages. The nice thing about mortgages is that the real estate is what is called *real property* and has value regardless of who owns it. If a borrower cannot pay the mortgage, the bank can take over ownership of the property and sell it to someone else who can pay. This is called *foreclosure* because the bank is closing out the loan before the life of the loan is up.

Mortgages are usually established for 15 or 30 years with the loan amount, the *principal,* being paid slowly over that period of time. If a borrower has trouble making the monthly installment payments, then foreclosure becomes a possibility. Of course this is not only bad for the borrower but bad for the bank as well, since finding another buyer will take time and then there is always the issue of sale price: will the bank get all their money back?

Banks are well aware of the risks in lending money on real estate, so they do several things to protect themselves. First, they appraise the property themselves so regardless of the sales price, they decide what the property is worth if they have to sell it. Next, they don't lend the full value of the property but some lesser amount resulting in what is called *loan-to-value.* For example, if the bank decides that a house is worth $100,000 they may only lend $75,000 on it, resulting in a loan-to-value of $75,000/$100,000 = 75%. In this way, if the mortgage fails, the bank will in all probability get their money back, which is the same as getting depositor's money back to keep the bank solvent.

The bank also looks at the borrower. If a mortgage fails it adds expense to the bank's operations. Banks want to operate as efficiently as possible and that means heading off bad loans. Banks routinely ask borrowers for detailed information on their ability to pay off the loan. Information the bank will want could be called a "stress" test. Are borrowers likely to lose their jobs, and if so how long will it take them to get re-employed? In the meantime, what savings do they have that will allow them to continue to pay their mortgage? Only after the bank has satisfied itself that the loan-to-value is more than enough to cover any possible loss, and that the borrower has a stable source of income and enough savings to cover any short-term upset, will the bank agree to the loan. This assessment of risk on the part of the bank is called *underwriting*.

Underwriting

Underwriting is a strange term and derives from the beginnings of the insurance industry. The legend is that merchants sitting in a coffee house in London, a coffee house presumably named Barclays, back in the 1700s, could look at a blackboard and see a list of ships with destinations, cargoes and captains listed alongside. If the merchants wanted to make some money, they would guarantee the success of the voyages or "insure" the voyages by writing their names underneath the voyages they were taking responsibility for. In return these merchants were paid what is called a *premium*. If the voyage was successfully completed the merchant was better off, having gained a premium. If the voyage failed, as in the ship and cargo was lost, then the merchant had to pay for the loss or some fraction of the loss. Naturally this would mean catastrophic loss, so merchants doing the insuring were very careful to assess the risks. Only after satisfying himself that the ship was sound, the cargo not likely to spoil and the captain highly experienced and successful did the merchant sign on for the risk by writing his name under the voyage (or "underwriting" as it came to be called) – assessing risk.

When banks finance mortgages they too do underwriting, assessing the risk of making loans. Houses are not likely to sink like ships, so the risk may appear to be limited, but there is fire. Banks require all the property used as collateral for their loans to be insured against fire. *Collateral* is the term used for assets pledged to guarantee a loan. For mortgages the collateral is the house.

Risk

Risk is not always so easy to assess as either risky or riskless. Most loans have different degrees of risk. Some borrowers, for example, may not really need the loan to buy a house but take out a loan because they can earn more interest on their money than they have to pay for a house loan. In such a case, the bank has not only the house for collateral but also the cash the borrower has otherwise invested. In this case, the borrower has more power in the relationship than the bank and may be pretty confident of getting a house loan from any bank at a lower rate.

Competition among banks drives down their interest rates as the various banks compete for mortgage business by offering lower interest rates. In a 5% mortgage rate environment, a low-risk borrower may be offered 4¾%. On the other hand, a young couple just starting out may have little savings and a need to buy their first house with an 85% loan-to-value. This is a much higher-risk loan so the bank may offer a higher interest rate loan, say 5½%. This seems unfair, but financial markets don't work very well if they are guided by other considerations besides profit.

For example, say that you had applied for a mortgage and were offered one at 7%. You would want an explanation. What if the explanation was that several existing mortgages were failing, so to help out the failing borrowers the bank was asking you to pay a higher rate? You might not think "fairness" was such a good idea under those circumstances. Neither would anybody else. The only way financial markets can do the most good for the greatest number of people is to hold everybody to the same standard. That standard is profit, regardless of where it comes from. So banks have not only a right but a duty to carefully underwrite their loans and charge an appropriate interest rate for each loan based on expectation of repayment.

In addition to lending money for mortgages, banks also make business loans. These types of loans are much trickier because usually collateral is in non-cash assets. Besides, the bank really doesn't want the collateral, they want the loan to be repaid so they can lend the money to someone else. Underwriting loans is what is called the *core competency* of bank underwriters. If a loan fails then the bank must try to make itself "whole" by selling the collateral and this is not a core competency of the bank – banks are in business to make loans, not to sell collateral assets. Making business loans puts the bank in a more precarious position because if a loan fails, the bank may find itself trying to sell collateral it has no idea who to sell to or what it is worth – it is not real property like real estate.

Underwriting business loans is much trickier; it usually means knowing a lot more about the borrower and starting out with small loans to see how the borrower performs on those. For financing business there are different kinds of banks called *Investment Banks* or *Merchant Banks*. As soon as you move from savings to investment, you move from banks to investment or merchant banks.

Because business loans are more problematic, banks are forced to look at the viability of a business and that means considering the strength of the company's products and the business cycle. The strength of the company's products will mostly be ascertainable from financial reports on sales and profitability. What the bank will look for is growing sales and growing profitability. If a company is growing and becoming more profitable it is viable, at least in the short term. But that is not the whole story – there is the *business cycle*.

The Business Cycle

There are many businesses competing with each other in all sectors of the economy. Naturally, each business thinks it is best and so assumes a market share for itself that is not always realistic. If all businesses do this then there will be over-production; and when too much of something is supplied, prices collapse. For example, if a bank can't make loans, it will reduce the interest rate until borrowers come in to borrow at attractive rates that are lower than what they are offered elsewhere. The cost of borrowing or raising money is called the *cost-of-capital*, or COC.

Theoretically, any project can be financed or any house purchased where the loan rate is lower than the expected return on the investment. If the COC of buying houses, for example, is lower than the expected return on home ownership, then many people will go out and take out loans to buy or build houses. Soon the housing market will be over-supplied and prices will fall; with falling prices the return on houses will fall below COC and housing purchases will stop. Some of the loans will fail, and in such a case the bank is unlikely to recover its loss. Accordingly, banks will have less money, so interest rates will rise, making the COC higher and making housing purchases even less attractive. This will lead to a housing slump and since housing is so central to our economy as a whole, the entire economy will suffer. It will take time for housing demand to pick up back to normal levels. This boom-to-bust in the housing market is called the *business cycle*.

The business cycle is not only in housing but in the economy in general. For example, in the late 1990s when the internet was going through rapid expansion, investors competed with each other to buy stock in internet companies, driving stock prices up to breathtaking levels. Of course, the limited supply of internet stocks meant that the competition drove prices up to levels way beyond what the companies could ever return to the investors in profit. Once this was realized by the investing public, the appetite for internet stocks fell and stock prices soon followed. Those investors who bought internet stocks took on big losses and so didn't have money to spend on other things, so the whole economy collapsed.

If interest rates remained high after a market collapse nobody would want to borrow any money to make purchases and there would be no way to revive the economy; even projects with expected good returns would not be able to assure returns above a high COC. This would be terrible – the economy would grind to a halt and stay there. There would be little employment and the collapse would continue into all sectors of the economy; there would soon be public disorder as people fought for food and a place to live. This is too terrible an outcome so the government steps in and reduces interest rates. A fall in COC then prompts new borrowings on profitable projects that provide employment, with wages to buy food and housing and profits for the lenders. Soon the overall economy is humming again, headed to the next roller-coaster ride: up in euphoria then down in panic. This is the business cycle.

You would think that grownups would be better-behaved than that, but when it comes to money, grownups are like the most spoiled brats you have ever seen. Haven't you noticed?

The Federal Reserve

In the United States we have the Federal Reserve system, which is an organization that doesn't so much set interest rates as cause interest rates to rise and fall on its metering the availability of money. After a general economic collapse the Federal Reserve takes actions to bring down interest rates. After the stock market internet "bubble" of the late 1990s the Federal Reserve brought down interest rates to close to zero; that started a housing boom that ended in another bust in 2008. People who had lost money in internet stocks – or "tech bubble" as it was called – then had an opportunity to make money in the housing boom and went at it with the same enthusiasm they had brought to buying internet stocks, with short memories evidently. Soon there were more houses than the population could possibly live in and the housing market collapsed. Those losses, widespread as they were, pretty much reduced spending down to very low levels and the economy collapsed again. Again the Federal Reserve – "The Fed" – took actions to bring down interest rates, so for five years interest rates have been near zero but with very little borrowing. This is what is meant by the business cycle, the cycling between boom and bust.

Near-Cash Assets

The nature of savings is typically what may be called *near-cash assets* because all you have to do is go to your bank and withdraw your money at any time. This easy and quick convertibility to cash earns them the classification as near-cash assets. This implies that assets can be measured in two ways: how much, and how quickly convertible to cash. And just as quantity is an analog value, anything from say 1 to 10, nearness to cash is also an analog value. For example, passbook savings can be withdrawn in a few minutes. Series EE U.S. Government savings bonds (zero-coupon bonds) may take a little longer to convert to cash. A bond issued by a company or a municipality will take several days to clear. If somebody pays you with a credit card, that will take several days and may not get you the money until the end of the month. So there are degrees of what may be called *liquidity*, which is the convertibility of an asset into cash.

Generally speaking, the more liquid an asset is, the less interest it pays or the less return it produces. Sometimes people want more interest than banks pay on passbook savings so they may purchase a CD (Certificate of Deposit) instead. In this instrument, the bank locks up your money for a fixed term and in return pays higher interest. If you demand the money back prematurely, you will get your money but will have to pay a penalty. Another way to increase the interest your money can earn is to buy a bond.

Bonds

A bond is a promise to pay a face amount at some point in the future. If the bond has a face value of $1000, and you paid $1000 for it, you can pretty much expect to turn the bond in for the face amount when the bond "matures," which may be in say five years. Over that period the bond would be expected to pay interest every six months at the rate documented on the bond as the *coupon*, the rate of interest. So a bond has three dimensions: face value, coupon and term. But some provision must be made for people who need to cash in their bonds before the term is up, maybe they have an emergency and need the money.

Essentially when you buy and sell bonds you are buying or selling a cash flow. The cash flow is the aggregate accumulation of the interest payments over the remaining term of the bond, plus the return of capital at the bond's expiration. So a 10-year 5% bond with a face value of $1000 will pay, typically, 20 interest payments of $25 (one every six months), and in ten years return the original $1000. If a bond holder needs to sell a bond during the 10-year term, the sale price will be set by the expected cash flow relative to the prevailing interest rate. The cash flow is $1000 at the expiration plus all the interest payments in between.

If at the time of the sale prevailing interest rates have risen to 7%, then a 5% bond is no longer worth its original amount because it only pays 5% in a 7% environment – nobody would buy such a bond, so it couldn't be sold. Upon encountering this unhappy news, the bond holder could just refuse to sell the bond and simply wait to collect the

$1000 face value. But what would be lost with that decision is the opportunity to make an additional 2% during the remaining term of the bond.

The difference between 5% and 7% on a $1000 ten-year bond is $500 vs. $700 in interest, a difference of $200. So $200 is prorated over the remaining life of the bond and subtracted from the face value to arrive at the fair market price for the bond. For example, with five years remaining on the term of the bond, half of its life, the $200 difference becomes $100, so the bond has a market value of $900 at the 5-year mark in a 7% environment. In the 10th year, at expiration, it is worth $1000, the expected cash flow to the owner of the bond at expiration.

Since interest rates are constantly fluctuating, bonds selling in the secondary market seldom trade at the face value but trade at a higher price "premium" or at a lower price "discount." There are other factors. Bonds are also issued by corporations, and the perceived ability to repay bondholders may fluctuate with changing business fortunes. Companies who experience improving business conditions see their bond prices rise in the market as expectation of repayment becomes more certain, adding to the attractiveness of the bond.

Although bonds issued by the federal government are very safe, they are still subject to price fluctuations caused by changing interest rates. A 5% bond is just not very attractive in a 7% environment and if you want to sell your bond it will not command the same face value. In this respect bonds are not near enough to cash to trade like cash; only passbook savings guarantee your original amount, with interest, on any day you want to cash in.

Savings, whether in the form of passbook savings, CDs, bonds or notes are all near-cash assets and thought to be a pretty safe place to put your money; they should not require much underwriting or assessing the risk of the institution on the saver's part. This is not to say some due diligence is not required; institutions do fail on occasion and savings that are protected by FDIC may well be earning a lower interest rate.

Some institutions, as a class, are thought to be safer and don't require FDIC guarantees. These are utilities issuing bonds, because utilities provide a service people can't do without, like electricity or water. But they do occasionally fail, taking savers' money with them. Municipalities issuing bonds are thought to be even safer because they have taxing authority and can always raise taxes to pay bondholders, but there are occasional municipal bankruptcies. The lower- risk bonds are those issued by the U.S. government in the form of bills, notes and bonds. The thesis here is that the

U.S. Government has both taxing authority and printing authority and as a last resort can always print more money to pay holders of what are commonly called Treasuries. Similar instruments issued by other countries are called *sovereign bonds*.

The United States of America is thought to be the safest currency provider in the world and for this reason is sometimes called the *reserve currency* because it is the alternative currency used around the world when the local currency is unacceptable. For example, if a Russian oligarch wants to buy a Mercedes-Benz in Kazakhstan, the local dealer might not accept Russian rubles and the Russian might not trust the Kazakhstan tenge, so they settle on U.S. dollars, generally accepted around the world.

Because of the perceived safety of U.S. dollars, other countries often put their surplus money to work by buying U.S. Treasuries with their reserves, money they don't need right away. In recent years the biggest buyers of U.S. Treasuries have been the countries of Japan and China. Since these two countries are export powerhouses, they have a lot of money in U.S. dollars particularly, and have put it all into U.S. Treasuries. As of the end of 2012, China holds $1.2 trillion in U.S. Treasuries and Japan holds $1.1 trillion. That is a massive amount of money.

Zero-Coupon Bonds

There is some bother associated with bonds in that bond issuers must mail out or otherwise transfer interest payments to bondholders, who must then deposit those interest payments and perhaps do some recordkeeping. As a workaround to this administrative burden, *zero-*

coupon bonds may be bought and sold instead. In a zero-coupon bond there is no coupon. Instead the bond is sold at a discount calculated to match the cash flow expected in a regular bond.

Looking at the $1000 bond already described above, the coupon cash flow for a 5% bond over ten years would be $500. So that same bond could be issued as a $1000 face value zero-coupon bond at an initial offering price of $500. If held to maturity, in ten years the bond holder would realize a $1000 payment. Sales during the interim period would be prorated like a regular bond.

Savings

When the term *savings* is used it refers to the act of putting money aside from immediate use and reserving it for future use. You could think of this as moving money from today into the future. And money may be moved in both directions. Money that is in the future may be moved to the present by means of a loan. In a loan we get money today that will be repaid with future earnings, so all we are doing is moving that future money back to the present. If we move today's money to the future, we are saving; if we move future money to the present, we are borrowing.

This seems easy enough, except that we haven't accounted for changing interest rates. Interest plays a role whenever you move money forwards or backwards – earning interest when moving money forward and paying interest when moving money backwards. Which again is not too difficult, except that prevailing interest rates may change, will change, over the term of the forward or backward movement.

Say, for example, that you obtain a $1000 ten-year loan at 5% and that over the life of the loan interest rates generally rise to around 8% when the loan is due. The money you will use to repay the loan will be from wages that were put into savings earning various increasing rates of interest up to 8%. Over a ten-year period, those accumulated savings may have earned say $300 in interest. So when the loan is repaid, the total outlay may have been $1500 but interest earned on savings was $300, so the net cost of the loan was $200 or 2%. Of course, things could have gone the other way and declining interest rates over the term of the loan might have resulted in only $100 of interest earned, resulting in a 4% loan repayment in a 3% interest rate environment.

Nominal Rate vs. Real Rate

What the above illustration attempts to show is that due to constantly changing interest rates, there are two interest rates associated with saving and borrowing – the nominal rate and the real rate. The *nominal rate* of interest is the coupon or the agreed-upon rate of interest when the loan is extended or the bond is purchased. The *real rate* of interest is that rate actually paid or earned over the term of the agreement. The real rate may be calculated by subtracting the prevailing rate from the coupon rate: for example, 5% coupon - 2% prevailing rate = 3% real rate. In this case, the coupon should be 2% but since the bond was purchased at a 5% coupon, the bondholder is better off but the company issuing the bond is worse off due to changes in interest rates. As a practical matter, it is seldom that the nominal rate equals the real rate over the term of the loan or bond, so some attention must be paid to the expected direction of interest rates.

Another way to think of the nominal vs. real rate is to think of expensive dollars and cheap dollars. A dollar today will not be worth a dollar in ten years. It could be worth more in a catastrophe that eliminated much productivity, making dollars more scarce in the future. But that would be quite a catastrophe, making the Great Depression of the 1930s look like a walk in the park by comparison. The opposite is the almost certain outcome, that of a dollar being worth less in ten years if only because we would rather have a dollar now than later, making the "now" dollar more valuable than the "later" dollar.

Since "now" dollars are more valuable, in most cases loans are a better deal for borrowers than lenders, because borrowers pay back expensive "now" dollars with cheaper "later" dollars. To compensate for that, lenders charge interest; but the interest is fixed on the day the loan is taken out, while interest will continue to fluctuate over the term of the loan, trending up or trending down. If interest rates trend up, then the real rate on the loan goes down because the dollars being used to repay the loan are getting cheaper faster than expected. If interest rates trend down, then the interest being paid is higher than the real rate and the loan becomes more expensive.

Interest rates are more or less controlled by the Fed; interest rates are pushed down during stagnant business conditions to prompt more borrowing to stimulate the economy. So a lowering of prevailing rate below your loan rate means the economy has declined since you took out your loan and if you took out a new loan, it would come at a lower interest rate.

It may be more realistic to substitute the rate of inflation in place of prevailing rate but the rate of inflation may not be known whereas the prevailing interest rate is well publicized, by banks trying to make loans, for example. But few borrowers consider inflation when taking out loans and just accept whatever interest rate the bank charges. The purpose of this book is to show you that the actual rate you pay is not the published rate. For example, if your boat springs a leak, you will have to bail. If you bail at a rate (inflation rate) faster than the leak (the bank-published interest rate) your boat floats, but if the leak is greater than your bailing rate, the boat sinks. Loans work the same way, there are two rates: repayment rate and inflation rate. Or to put it another way, life has leaks in it and you had better start bailing.

The Components of Interest Rate

As we have already seen, interest rates change over time so it may be useful to see how interest rates are arrived at and what prompts changes in interest rates. While there are multiple explanations of the components that make up an interest rate, they all fall under four general areas:

1. Time Value of Money – convenience of having money now rather than later.

2. Risk – risk that the lender will not get fully repaid.
3. Liquidity - risk that the loan will be repaid early or late.
4. Inflation – risk that repayment dollars will be cheaper than loan dollars.

The time value of money is simply that it is more convenient to have money in the present rather than in the future simply because you may need it.

Risk is calibrated up or down depending on the perceived certainty of repayment. Generally, debt instruments issued by the U.S. government are considered close to risk-free and so carry a very low if not nil contribution to aggregate interest rate. And since liquidity is generally not a problem for the U.S. government, since Treasuries are in great demand, the remaining component of Treasury interest rates must be inflation.

Debt instruments of other issuers don't normally come with those Federal caveats, so all three components of interest rate calculation play a role. Risk of course is risk and requires little explanation – some borrowers are simply better risks. The better the risk the borrower is the lower the rate that borrower will pay for a loan. Of course risk is also hedged with collateral and with insurance. If a borrower becomes incapacitated, how will the loan be repaid? That is where collateral plays a role, or the borrower may be insured to cover personal incapacity.

The liquidity issue seems like a non-issue but is an issue. Early repayment burdens the lender with a need to find another qualified borrower. This is sometimes not easy, so early repayment means loss of a reliable cash-flow that required some expense on the part of the lender to arrange. For a lender, liquidity risk may also mean that repayment is late rather than early, so the cash cannot be quickly redeployed into a better-performing debt instrument.

Inflation

The final component of interest rate is inflation. To quote Milton Friedman, a famous Nobel-prize winning economist from the

University of Chicago, *"...Inflation is always and everywhere a monetary phenomenon."* In other words, the amount of things that a dollar buys does not rise dramatically from period to period because those things are the result of productivity, of man and machine, and those are items that just don't grow very rapidly. What can grow very rapidly is the money supply, as the Fed decreases interest rates and ramps up purchasing debt instruments in the open market – presto, you have more money in circulation. As sellers perceive there is more money for the same amount of goods and services, they raise prices thinking that with the extra money supply, people will not be all that reluctant to pay a little bit more. They are right, people are less sensitive to price as their personal money supply rises. A $100 gift will not be spent with the same care as $100 earned and saved over time. This is because the $100 gift was obtained for doing nothing, while the $100 earned and saved took a lot of work.

In a high-inflation environment the utility of those things a dollar buys remains relatively flat. For example, the utility of a car or a toaster, or a house or a steak remains pretty much the same. We would love to have a steak for dinner and drive to the steakhouse in a new car, but those pleasures are not much affected by time. I could put off both the steak and the car without much hardship, knowing in the end I will get them both and will enjoy them both whenever they come. So the increased money supply is not matched by either increased productivity or increased utility, and prices rise to absorb the extra money in circulation.

During periods of high inflation a lot more money will be needed, and this makes the money you have less valuable – it buys less. Think about postage stamps. When I was 8 years old, it cost 3¢ to mail a first-class letter. Today the same letter costs 49¢ to mail within the U.S. The rise over 63 years from 3¢ to 49¢ represents an inflation rate of 4.55% per year. Dollar bills have not changed in appearance from those I used as an 8-year-old, except they were a lot scarcer then. But back then for $1 I could have mailed 33 letters and had a penny left over. Today $1 will only mail two letters. So $1 mailed 33 letters in 1952 and mails two letters in 2013. That is a dramatic drop in value for the U.S. dollar due to inflation.

The Rule of 72

This is a good time to present the "rule of 72." If you divide an interest or inflation rate into the number 72 the answer will be, in years, the time it takes for an investment to double in value or to get cut in half in value by inflation. So if you take an interest rate of 3% and divide 3 into 72, you will learn that an investment at 3% will double in 24 years. Similarly, at an annual inflation rate of 3% money will lose half of its value in 24 years. So $1 invested at 3% over 24 years will then become $2, but that $2 will have the purchasing power of $1 due to inflation. You are right back where you started from after 24 years!

That is not much fun, so what many people do is try to get a return on their savings that beats inflation. Say that you realized a return of 6% over a 24-year period of 3% inflation. In 24 years, as we have seen, a 3% inflation rate will cut your savings in half. But a growth rate of 6% over 24 years according to the rule of 72 will double after only 12 years and will double again after another 12 years. So $1 invested at 6% over 24 years becomes $4 that will have $2 in purchasing power at a 3% inflation rate. At 6% you have doubled your real purchasing power from $1 to $2. This is the core idea of beating inflation.

Chapter 3

Inflation

AFTER WWI THE VICTORS, France and Britain, through the Versailles Treaty imposed on the loser, Germany, a crushing set of conditions that Germany was unable to survive. Reparations payments were set very high and some of Germany's most productive factories were taken from her. The combination of high payments and reduced output capacity resulted in a shortage of currency, which the German state attempted to correct for by simply printing more money.

There were many personal stories of hardship during this period, but perhaps none portrays the life more clearly than the story of a concert pianist wishing to be paid in sausages because the currency that would be used to pay him instead was worth many sausages on the evening of the recital, but only worth a few sausages the next day when he would arrive at the sausage store. This is called *inflation* and in this particular case, *hyperinflation*.

Inflation is caused by two conditions. One is people perceiving a decline in the value of the currency and so demanding more currency to cover their anticipated loss (the hyperinflation of Germany in 1921). The other cause of inflation is people perceiving there is a lot more money in circulation and naturally wanting more than usual since it is so available (Spain after the discovery of gold in the New

World). In either case, inflation is, as Milton Friedman stated, *"...always and everywhere a monetary phenomenon."*

Man with German Deutsch Marks
(1921-1924)

Spanish Gold from the New World

But inflation is also something else that Milton Friedman didn't bring up, but the key founder of our country, James Madison, did: loss of confidence in the currency. With the transition from British colony with the highly coveted British pound sterling currency to independent American country with no currency, the Revolutionary colonial government had to finance the revolution; this was done with the creation of the first national currency, *continentals*. But the people lost faith in the continental and the continental fell in purchasing power; soon the expression *"Not worth a continental,"* came into general use to describe anything that had no value. The first U.S. currency collapsed, not because of inflation but due to loss of confidence. To accept a substitute for gold, you have to believe in the person, or people, doing the substituting. At the time of the American war for independence, there was little confidence that the new nation would prevail and so little confidence in the currency it was issuing.

As we saw in the chapter on savings, gold started out as the medium of exchange and became money. Then, for convenience, receipts for gold became money. This eventually led to the federal government taking on the responsibility for managing a national currency. The dollar bill then became a receipt for gold, easily transferable, available in many denominations and all backed by gold on deposit owned by the federal government. Continentals were not backed by gold.

The good thing about being on a "gold standard" is that gold is not readily available but must be mined and then refined; that takes so much work that often gold mines go unworked because they are not profitable. So gold is rare, therefore a generally desired commodity, and therefore a reliable store of value; since not much is mined from year to year, it is therefore a stable foundation for value.

There are problems with a gold standard. If there are wars, there is general loss of confidence and that means loss of confidence in the currency. That prompts a flight to safety, and that means a flight to gold – the ultimate currency. In such circumstances, gold paper receipts are no longer good enough, people want the real thing. With the increased demand, gold prices rise to reconcile supply with demand. If the dollar is a receipt for gold, then suddenly that dollar is worth a lot more money, and prices would fall to accommodate the new higher intrinsic valuation of the dollar receipt for gold. By taking the dollar off the gold standard this problem goes away.

Then there is another source of appreciation in gold – production. If mining is not successful there is less gold, and lack of supply drives up gold prices. You can imagine the challenge our economy would have in trying to keep a lid on the price of gold in order to maintain orderly markets; after all, shouldn't say a quart of milk, which comes from a very regular supply, maintain a steady price? This may be difficult under a gold standard.

The Great Depression of the 1930s spawned much thinking about the nature of money, and after WWII and the end of the depression the industrial nations got together and adopted the Bretton Woods agreement on the gold standard. The U.S. dollar was given a value of 1/35 of an ounce of gold, and global currencies were convertible to the U.S. dollar at that valuation. This of course was a straightjacket that would prove at some point to be very inconvenient. That point of inconvenience was reached in 1971, at which time U.S. President Richard Nixon took the U.S. dollar off the gold standard. That meant that the U.S. dollar was no longer a receipt for gold and became *fiat currency*, currency because we say it is.

The last time we had a fiat currency it was the continental, and that didn't do so well. But as James Madison pointed out, the problem is confidence, not gold. Today, as the world's only superpower, the United States inspires confidence and that props up the U.S. dollar as the currency of last resort, globally. So in this case, with the printing of vast amounts of currency ordered by the Federal Reserve to stimulate the economy, inflation has not occurred because despite the supply of U.S. Dollars, there is still confidence in the currency. Friedman would have been surprised, I'm sure. But his opposite, John Maynard Keynes, would also have been surprised. According to Keynes, the supply of money should have stimulated the economy; but it didn't, or at least didn't in the proportion anticipated. Instead, the law formulated by Jean-Baptiste Say seems to fit better: workers who work to meet the demands of others then demand products to meet their demands, so full employment creates a full and circular economy. Problems arise when there is an imbalance or oversupply of an unwanted product, which if a market is perfectly free would be rare.

The study of economics, within which the study of inflation is conducted, makes one fundamental assumption: man is naturally incentivized to acquire wealth. Just as an example, let's say you were offered, for the identical work, a wage in one case of $10/hour and in the other case, $15/hour. Which job would you take? How many people do you know who would prefer to work for $10/hour when they could be paid $15/hour for the same work? This preference for greater value is the bedrock of the study of the economic behavior of mankind, otherwise known as Economics.

In physics this same law is applied to electricity in the observation that electricity always takes the path of least resistance. The same law applies to economics in that people may also be relied upon to always choose the path of least resistance, from selecting the shortest route to drive between two points to trying to find the closest parking place to a store entrance.

The concept of overtime pay is rooted in this phenomenon, to manage the tradeoff between gaining wealth while maximizing leisure. People prefer leisure over work, but go to work to support the maximum amount of leisure – it is a tradeoff.

The general consensus is that people will be satisfied to work 40 hours over a 5-day workweek in order to enjoy two days of leisure over what has come to be called the weekend. If given the opportunity to work more hours at their base wage most people will refuse, preferring to enjoy their leisure time instead. So if an employer has more work than workers, he has the choice of hiring another worker or paying a higher wage for work performed after the regular work day or workweek. This is called *overtime*. Most employers will pay overtime until the amount of overtime equals the wage of an additional worker, at which point a new worker will be added. The workers who were working overtime were convinced to give up their leisure by being offered overtime wages, perhaps half again as much as their base wage for the overtime hours worked. The employees don't wish to give up their leisure but see in the higher wage an opportunity to improve their condition at a level higher than the leisure time given up. It is not just the leisure vs. higher-pay trade-off that is subject to people's calculations – almost every decision people make will require a calculation of value that will result in a choice.

Time is Money

In many if not all of these calculations time will be part of the equation – there will be money and there will be time. And as it turns out, time is a partner to money, giving rise to the expression *"the time value of money."* Would you rather have a dollar now, or later? Just as almost everybody prefers a $15/hour wage over a $10/hour wage, so almost everybody would rather have a dollar now than later. Therefore, since a dollar now is more desirable than a dollar later, it is more valuable. In order to equalize the proximate and more distant dollars, the more distant dollar is made larger – would you rather have a dollar now or a dollar plus 5 cents a year from now? Some may prefer to wait to acquire an extra nickel. This is the time value of money.

Another way to look at the time value of money is to see that money loses value with time. A dollar a year from now is not equal to a dollar now, so a nickel must be added to it to make it equal with today's dollar. That means that our dollar has lost value over time. This is called *inflation*, because we have to inflate tomorrow's dollar to make it equal to today's dollar. We can use the word *inflation* because it implies that no value is really being added, it is all just air. And so it is: $1.05 next year is equal to $1.00 today, the only difference being that we have added a nickel; the nickel has not increased the value of the dollar, it has only made it equal to today's dollar.

When interest rates are set at banks, a calculation must be made on what the time value of money is. Expected rate of inflation is a key determinant but not the only determinant. Other factors are the risk that the loan will not be repaid (risk) or that the loan will not be repaid on time (liquidity). Banks routinely use underwriting to assess the creditworthiness of the borrower and assign to each an interest rate for one of several classifications of borrowers. And collateral will be required, like holding the deed to a house for a mortgage, but this is a backstop; the bank really doesn't want the house.

In opening a passbook savings account, the bank is the borrower and offers a lower interest rate largely due to the lower risks associated with loans to banks versus loans to individuals.

Certificates of Deposit (CDs) offer higher interest, but in this case it is not the change in risk profile of the bank that is the driver, it is liquidity. In a CD, higher interest is offered for agreeing not to demand the money back before a published term of time. Now the bank has a much more certain deposit and is willing to pay more for it because the bank can make a much more certain profit on it.

So interest rates are largely calculated from convenience, inflation, risk and liquidity. Risk and liquidity are typically adjustments made over and above convenience and expected inflation.

Inflation is constantly changing, largely driven by the business cycle and the Federal Reserve's response to the impact the business cycle is having on employment. Keeping unemployment below 6% is a main objective of Federal Reserve policy. When unemployment is pushing up over 6%, the Fed takes steps to reduce interest rates thus prompting borrowing, much of which goes into business expansion that will then employ workers.

As long as the added money going into the economy is accompanied by productivity that produces more goods and services, the additional money is absorbed by the added goods and services and there is no inflation – a dollar is a dollar. But when Spanish ships began bringing back gold from the New World, there was no commensurate increase in Spanish production of goods and services – after all, factors of production were limited, so production in Spain stayed pretty much at the same level regardless of how much gold came into the country. So how was all this new gold to be absorbed by a flat economy? Higher prices. Just the presence of additional money prompted merchants to demand more for the goods and services that were available and a spiral of inflation was begun. A key point is that the goods and services are really no different than they were before the inflation, so the new higher price is not a reflection of product value but rather of currency devaluation. Pesetas were not worth as much after the influx of new gold.

Had the additional gold been the result of increased production within Spain, the additional money would have been absorbed by the additional product and the peseta would have continued unchanged in value.

Economic Expansion

When people become aware of inflation they accelerate their purchases, hoping to avoid paying higher prices with the more valuable money they have earned in the past. The dollar they earned is worth a dollar, but the dollar they will spend later is only worth 95¢ because prices have gone up. To avoid this, people buy today what could be postponed in order to make the most of their wages and savings.

If the opposite occurred and the supply of money fell, then a declining supply of money would have to cover a larger supply of goods and services, and prices would have to drop to support the movement of goods and services throughout the economy.

But when people become aware that there is deflation, and goods and services are getting cheaper, they postpone their purchase in the expectation that by waiting, prices will go even lower. Unlike a state of inflation that accelerates purchasing and therefore economic activity, deflation stops purchasing and economic activity. Deflation eventually leads to growing unemployment and in extreme cases to public disorder.

Given the choice between deflation and inflation, the Federal Reserve takes steps to prompt an annual inflation rate of 2% to 3% to keep the economy humming. This rate of inflation keeps everybody happy; workers see their wages rising and merchants see their prices rising, so purchasing and production are in sync and everybody feels slightly richer.

But as we have noted, inflation reduces the value of currency so attention has to be paid to savings, which will erode just with time from inflationary effects.

Usually inflation is contained within a nation-state; for example, the rate of inflation in the U.S. will be different than the rate of inflation in say Canada, or Great Britain, or France or Germany. Nevertheless, within the borders of a country the rate of inflation will be pretty much nationwide. In the U.S. we track inflation using the CPI (Consumer Price Index), which is generally thought to be a "market basket of goods and services" a typical family buys on a regular basis. As merchants and various vendors raise their prices to consumers in response to price hikes they see from inventory and services they must purchase, the price hikes are tracked in the CPI.

The CPI is also often used to set wages. Typically, workers will expect an annual raise from their employers in an acknowledgement of the necessity to keep pace with inflationary forces. Most employers also use the occasion of the annual raise to reward those employees who have performed at an outstanding level; those employees may expect a raise that may be a percent or two above the CPI rate of inflation. In a 3% rate of inflation environment outstanding employees may see a 4% or even 5% raise.

Wages and Inflation

Over a lifetime of work, an outstanding employee may see a wage growth rate of perhaps 4% or possibly even 5%, but in a 3% inflation environment the real purchasing power of earnings growth will be modest. For one thing, inflation is not the only influence on purchasing power – there are macro effects like localized real-estate markets growing at much faster rates in trendy locales or the opposite, losing value in declining neighborhoods.

Various goods and services will suffer the same variability in advance and decline due to changes in the competitive landscape. Occupations rise and fall on a sea of consumer sentiment. Exports and imports change, affecting the price of discrete goods and services. The overall U.S. economy in relation to other players in global markets will fluctuate. At one time, in the 1950s, there was a popular expression for U.S. consumer economics: "The American Dream." This was a level of prosperity that would give every hard-working family a house with a white picket fence, a garage and a car inside the garage. Those days are gone, and the U.S. standard of living has been on a straight-line decline ever since. The typical American family cannot buy today what it could in the 1950s, despite wages that kept pace with inflation.

So while working diligently is certainly important and expected to earn wages that keep pace with inflation, the real growth in wages comes from promotions to higher levels of responsibility that may see a much more dramatic raise in personal wage rates. Nevertheless, those higher wages don't necessarily come with freedom from economic pressure. Often higher wages are accompanied by higher spending, and the savings rate may not be improved at all. And it is the savings that will largely determine family fortunes like sending kids to college and enjoying a secure retirement.

Just to give an example, let's say in a particular family Mom and Pop both work. Over a lifetime of work, say 40 years, the average household income has been $100,000 per year. That sounds like a lot, but over 40 years that adds up to just $4,000,000. Now take a savings rate of 5% of gross income, which doesn't often happen, but say it does in this case; 5% of $4 million is $200,000. Well, college for two kids will likely take $100,000, so that leaves Mom and Pop to retire on $100,000. I'm afraid they won't get very far. Even a family that has been paid double those wages, and saved at the same rate, won't make it. This is a real problem but one for which there is a solution – investing savings in the stock market.

Inflation is constant, so a 3% annual rate of inflation is really 3/12ths of 1% on a monthly basis. But it is inconvenient and a lot more work to adjust for inflation monthly, so it is usually an annual adjustment; in some cases it may be an adjustment that occurs every few years instead. For example, postal rates change about every two years, up from a five-year interval back in the 1950s. Barbers and manicurists could adjust pricing each day, but competitive forces generally dictate more periodic adjustments like two years, or longer in more competitive markets. Gasoline prices change almost daily, which is surprising given the large storage capacity available to store gasoline. The gas you buy today was probably refined months or even a year earlier. This demonstrates that it is not production cost that drives price, it is market competition, and much of that competition is subject to inflation and the expectation of inflation.

Staying Ahead of Inflation

The most fluid pricing, however, is in the stock market, where change occurs every few seconds as millions of buyers and sellers come together to buy and sell stocks. Perhaps for this reason, the stock market is a very reliable inflation monitor, and putting your savings into the stock market is perhaps the surest way to keep it from getting eaten up by inflation. In fact, S&P 500 long-term annualized return is between 9½% and 11½%, which is well ahead of inflation and is the solution to saving for the future.

If wage growth is 1% to 2% above inflation, and the S&P 500 is 6½% to 8½% above inflation, that is a spread of 5% to 7%. So, compounding $1000 at an annualized wage growth rate of 5% over 30 years produces $4,321, while $1000 compounded over the same period at an S&P 500 equivalent rate of 10% produces $17,449. That is more than four times the growth of inflation. That is the power of time and the stock market and the reason that while earning good wages is important, it is a rigorous savings and investment program that will determine how well you survive what life throws at you.

Chapter 4

Investing in Companies

BANKS TAKE IN DEPOSITORS' money and lend it out for mortgages, business loans and other uses, for profit. From the borrower's perspective, the money is a loan with a fixed repayment amount – a fixed rate of interest and a fixed term for repayment. Everything is fixed in advance with loans and bonds so they are called *fixed* instruments. Investments vary in value with fortune and time and are therefore not fixed, but *variable* – variable financial instruments. So there are both "fixed" and "variable" financial instruments.

In loans, since the borrower has more money with the proceeds from the loan, the borrower is in a stronger cash position, so this additional purchasing power is called *leverage*. We use levers in a hammer, for example, to extract nails from wood. Another example of leverage is using a wrench to turn a nut. We can't turn a nut with our fingers, but if we use a wrench we can turn the nut; if it is hard to turn we can just use a longer wrench – this is leverage. Money is like a wrench: it gives us the power to do things we couldn't otherwise do without the borrowed money, so we have leverage thanks to money.

Debt vs. Equity

If we have savings, we have a choice in deciding between debt and equity, in acquiring a new bicycle, for example. Say you saw a bicycle you wanted but didn't want to spend your savings. You might share the cost and the ownership with a friend – you pay half and he or she pays the other half. If you are on different schedules this might work out, but there will inevitably be conflicts. Giving up ownership is sometimes hard to do, so you might decide to get a loan instead to buy the bicycle. In this case, the bike is all yours, and you have something you didn't have before. So you are leveraged, but at a cost – you have to make those loan payments.

Deciding between giving up ownership and taking on a loan is something that people and businesses are forced to think about every day. What most people and businesses do is decide on a combination of both – some borrowing and some forfeiting of ownership. We have already used the term *debt* to describe borrowing. The term for ownership is *equity*. If we have savings, we have the choice between buying a bicycle outright or giving up ownership, where we are giving up equity in that bike. We have to share but there are no loan payments on it – no debt.

If you buy a house, the bank will require a down payment of say 20%. If the house is appraised at $100,000 and you put down $20,000, the bank will lend you the remaining $80,000 to purchase the house. When you move in, the house presumably is worth $100,000; since you owe $80,000 on it, your equity in the house is $20,000. So the house is both debt and equity. If the house appreciates over time, your equity will grow since you are the owner and you get all the equity interest in the house. If, for example, gold was discovered on the property worth say a $1 million, the bank would still be entitled to $80,000 and no more. You, the equity interest holder, on the other hand now have equity of $1,020,000.

All increase of value is equity and that goes to the owner. For this reason, equity is not a fixed-income position but a "variable" position which rises and falls with the business cycle. Very few people or businesses have enough money to own the enterprise outright, so most families and businesses are combinations of debt and equity – debt to finance an equity position, and equity for growth. Families have houses and businesses have factories and machines with which to make things. In both cases, there is both debt and equity.

Capital Structure

Businesses can vary in size from what are called "Mom 'n Pop" establishments all the way up to huge multinational conglomerates like GE that has close to $150 billion in annual revenue. But in both cases, the enterprise is financed with debt and equity in what is called *capital structure*. This term refers to the relative weight of debt and equity. For example, GE has a debt-to-equity ratio of 2.40; that means that for every dollar of equity ownership there is in GE, $2.40 is owed to banks and individuals. You could say that GE is highly leveraged, but if they are profitable, that borrowed money is making money and the profits don't have to be shared with so many people, as long as the loan payments are made.

Another iconic American company operating all over the world is Procter & Gamble, makers of soaps and other household products. P&G has a debt-to-equity ratio of about .5, meaning for every dollar of equity owned, only 50¢ is owed to lenders. This makes P&G a more lightly leveraged company. Deciding on how to balance the capital structure is a decision made by the CEO (Chief Executive Office), the CFO (Chief Financial Officer), the Board of Directors and the lenders the company uses for borrowing or increasing their leverage.

If the company does not want to increase their leverage and they want money to grow the business, they can always give up equity or ownership in the company by issuing shares of stock. For Mom 'n Pop this could be a problem, but for GE or P&G this is not a big problem because they have thousands of owners who can prove their ownership with shares of stock. Since these companies have so many owners and anybody can be an owner by just buying some stock in the company, we call this type of ownership *public ownership* – these are "public" companies. Mom & Pop companies are privately owned companies; in other words, if Mom and Pop had given up some equity in their business, then you could say the business is *closely held*.

Well, you might think that if you owned some shares of GE, you would then be an owner and you might go to the headquarters and demand a summer job and maybe a new bicycle to go with it; after all, the company is profitable and you are an owner. You probably won't get too far. You see, there are thousands of owners and some of those owners own thousands of shares of stock. Also, the company is incorporated with bylaws that state that the owners have put the Board of Directors in charge; as a minority interest owner, you leave it up to the Board of Directors to run your business for you which they are required to do for your benefit. You are then entitled to your share of all the profits, and you can vote on various issues that come before the board, but your voice is small.

Most stock holders don't take an ownership interest in running the company but just buy the stock because they think the company is well managed and will continue to be profitable, causing their stock to appreciate in value.

Also, share ownership has advantages over direct ownership. If the company you have shares in gets into trouble and goes bankrupt, owing millions of dollars to creditors, your liability ends with your stock holdings. You can lose your stock, but no more. Creditors have no claims on the stockholders of the company beyond the stock they hold. If a Mom & Pop business gets into trouble and winds up owing millions of dollars to creditors, Mom and Pop may be personally liable for repayment. Public companies are "incorporated" and that limits the liability of the owners to the loss of their stock holdings and no more.

As we have described, companies have two ways to raise money: debt or equity. To use debt, they just go to their bankers and ask for a loan, or they can issue bonds to the public. In either case, as soon as the debt is added to, their monthly debt repayment goes up and they have to make those payments or else. Alternatively, the company can issue more shares of stock and just increase ownership of the enterprise. This brings in new money and will not trigger bigger monthly debt repayment.

Often existing owners don't like to see more stock issued because it decreases their share of ownership in what is called *dilution*, diluting their ownership. But the ownership is given up for an inflow of cash, so the existing owners just have a smaller share of a bigger pie and they have nothing to complain about.

Whether an enterprise uses debt or equity to raise money, the choice will usually be decided on their current capital structure, too much or too little debt, and the relative cost of debt vs. equity.

If interest rates are very low, due to the business cycle, it may be better to borrow at low interest rates. If on the other hand, and again due to the business cycle, the company's stock is trading at very high valuation in the stock market, well then maybe it is smarter to issue more shares, bringing in a bigger fraction of money for giving up a smaller fraction of ownership. So capital structure and market dynamics together will pretty much decide between debt and equity on any new money raising.

In the chapter on savings we discussed debt as a way to save money. Passbook savings are a debt the bank owes to the depositor for money the bank uses to loan out for profit. As we have discussed, companies have a choice whether to issue debt or equity for raising cash to finance operations. If the company chooses debt, then bonds will be issued; investors can buy bonds and earn interest on those bonds.

One disadvantage of bonds, however, is that their face value floats on the market, which may cause the face value to rise or to fall, mostly on interest rate changes but also on the reputation of the company issuing the bonds. If the company comes out with an exciting new product, you might see a rise in the value of your bond as demand for the company's bonds pick up. If bad news comes out on the company, bond prices will fall and your bond will be worth less.

When you buy a company's bonds, the company becomes your debtor, and they owe you not only the money you have lent to them but interest on that money as well. But you have a choice between lending the company money for interest, or buying shares in the company and becoming an owner, in which case you don't get interest, you get a share of the profit.

Capital Gain

If you own shares and the company comes out with an exciting new product, the value of the shares will rise and in some cases rise quite a bit, much more than any appreciation you will see in a bond. The reason for this is that bond prices adjust up and down to adjust the interest rate on the bond. For example, say a $1000 bond pays 5% interest or $50 per year. That $50 is called the *coupon* and doesn't change– you have purchased a cash flow. If the company introduces an exciting new product, suddenly there is less risk in loaning the company money so the company pays less interest to borrow. So any new bonds the company might issue will carry only a 4½% coupon or $45 a year. You will continue to receive your coupon of $50, so your bond is worth more than the new bonds.

If you want to sell your bond, which is identical to the new bonds except for the larger coupon it pays, you are going to want more money for it. You don't have to figure it out, the bond market will do it for you and you sell your bond you will be happy to learn that somebody bought it for $1050. The extra $50 is the added $5 per year in coupon the bond earns, multiplied by the 10 year remaining term of the bond: $50.

When you elect to own rather than lend, you buy shares of *common stock* in the company that then entitles you to a share in the profits. And when the company announces the exciting new product, not only do bond prices rise but share prices of common stock rise as well; but the stock price is not tied to interest rates so it may rise much more dramatically. This is called *capital gain*.

For example, say the common stock of the company with the exciting new product was trading for $50 per share before the announcement; after the announcement the stock price might rise to $60. This is a much more dramatic rise in stockowners' fortunes over the fortunes of bond holders. A $10 rise on a $50 stock is a 20% gain. A $50 rise on a $1000 bond is a 5% gain.

What if the company news being announced is bad news? What happens then? Pretty much the reverse: stockholders will see the value of their stock decline perhaps by 20% while bondholders will see the value of their bonds decline by perhaps 5%. From an investor's point of view, this is the difference between equity and debt.

But there is more to it. Over the 10-year life of the bond, the amount of appreciation will be limited by interest rates. The rise in the price of common stock is unlimited, so it would not be at all unusual to see stock price double over a 10-year period. So for what could be substantial capital gain, many people prefer the stock market over the bond market. But many people put their money in both in what could be called personal attention to capital structure.

Investing vs. Saving

Bonds are considered safer than stock because the only way you won't get your money back is if the company goes bankrupt. If the company remains solvent, at the expiration of the term of your bond you will get full face value back. This is not the case with common stock that may decline quite dramatically in price while the company remains solvent. Why would the stock price decline? Well, if the fortunes of the company didn't look so rosy, investors might lose interest in the stock and the price might collapse for lack of demand. Or maybe a new competitor to the company you are invested in has just come on the market with an exciting product that is much better than the product your company makes; well then, owners will abandon the old company and invest in the new. The old company's stock price will fall and the new company's stock price will rise.

This is very distressing for people who just want to invest and forget about it, and calls attention to the need for underwriting on the part of investors in common stock – except it isn't called underwriting in the stock market, it is called "investing" and includes a wide array of research initiatives to arrive at a go/no go decision. But much of this research can be dispensed with because companies come in all risk categories. There are many that have been in business a very long time, over 100 years, and are very unlikely to see their stock price decline by very much, if at all. In fact, by far the most likely outcome is a doubling of stock price every 10 years.

As we have discussed earlier, companies that wish to raise money from the public by issuing common stock shares are called *public* companies. In the total global market for common shares there are about 40,000 public companies. Some of these companies have been in business for many years and are so big and strong that they have little competition. Of course, that alone doesn't mean a good investment because people change and yesterday's favorite product is today's throw-away. For example, look at automobiles. If a car company didn't continually bring out exciting new models it would soon be out of business. Oldsmobile used to be the most innovative division of General Motors. Today Oldsmobile is only a memory for some and General Motors, once the largest, most prominent U.S. corporation, has gone through bankruptcy.

The GM Story

Owners of GM, which is to say stock holders, saw their shares go to zero as the company was reorganized and were issued new shares of common stock for a new GM. Those shares today are trading at about $33 per share (August 8, 2014).

What about the holders of the old shares, what happened to them? They lost their entire investment in GM, once the world's most respected company and despite the fact that from the government's point of view, GM was too big to fail. Apparently while GM was not allowed to fail, stockholders in GM were allowed to fail.

There are about 125 million investors in U.S. equity issues of common stock. If no one wants to buy GM stock, the stock theoretically will go to zero as some owners will want to cash in their shares at any price because they need the money for some emergency. Cashing out at any price will overwhelm buyers with sellers and will eventually drive the stock to zero.

But the company is still there. The company was recapitalized with government money, and today the new GM stock shares are trading; in fact, around 11,000,000 GM shares trade daily, causing the price to fluctuate daily by no more than around 30¢ on a $33 stock, or about 1%.

Make no mistake, the old GM did collapse. There was no interest on the part of prospective new investors in owning a piece of a failing company and the old GM went to zero. Stockholders were understandably upset about losing their money and thought they should be reimbursed by somebody, but they forgot they were owners and therefore liable for the decline of the company's shares. But there were also creditors who were owed millions of dollars, but shareholders' liability did not include debts of the company – shareholders' liability is limited to the cost of their shares; that is what a company is, a limited liability enterprise.

But stockholders do bear some responsibility. Through annual stock holder meetings, stock holders are given a chance to meet with the CEO and the board and discuss the performance of the company. If the stockholders are unhappy they can force action. How powerful investor groups are is open to speculation, but in any case, investors are owners and can't throw up their hands and say they are not responsible for the companies they own.

Most investors don't take an ownership interest and just acquire and dispose of the stock based on their understanding of the company's future prospects. The angry GM stockholders who lost their investments should have sold out when signals of distress at the company first came into view. From mid-2007 to May of 2009, or about 24 months, GM stock price declined over 90%, from $40 to $3.

In 1988, Ross Perot, a very successful businessman who had sold his company to GM, publicly criticized GM management for failing to exploit the company's assets to grow the company. The management seemed more focused on furnishing their offices. At the time of the bankruptcy, it was generally agreed that Ross had spoken the truth and when the U.S. government decided to save GM, but not its stock holders, they forced out the sitting CEO, Rick Wagoner. Evidently his inside knowledge of the company was considered irrelevant in turning the company around. A new CEO was named as a condition for a government bailout.

When I was in college, I had a friend who worked for GM. He told me a story about a GM sales executive who was visiting a distant city. The practice was to put a refrigerator in his hotel room so if he was hungry in the middle of the night, he could get up and get a sandwich and a beer. On this occasion they couldn't fit the refrigerator through the hotel room door, so they hired a crane and moved the refrigerator in through the window. I don't know if this story is true or not, but the person telling me this story believed it and so did I. This type of behavior may occur in companies that don't have competition, and they are done in by themselves rather than outsiders.

Now, you may think that GM had competition in Ford and Chrysler (this was before the German, Japanese, Korean, French and Swedish invasion), but they were not competitors – each auto company had its market of GM buyers, Ford buyers or Chrysler buyers; there wasn't much competition to it.

Be careful of companies that don't have competitors to discipline them. People are people and without incentive they get lazy. In business this is deadly because it happens so slowly nobody notices until one day the company is bankrupt. And at GM it wasn't only the executives taking big salaries and fixing up their offices, the labor unions made demands in wages and work rules that were unsustainable. GM was a case where the company (stockholders) was being robbed by management <u>and</u> labor.

Good Management vs. No Management

So if GM, at one time the world's greatest company, went bankrupt, what hope is there for investing in companies without losing your money? Well, the GM story is a cautionary tale of arrogance and apathy, but the fate of GM investors is not as difficult to avoid as you might suppose.

When I heard the story of the refrigerator being moved in through a window by crane so a GM executive could to get a beer and a sandwich in the middle of the night, I was justifiably put off by such arrogant behavior, and that just would have been one metric in my evaluation of GM as an investment. Also, I have always viewed labor unions as the instigators of excess throughout the companies they worked for. Where management failed to reign in the unions, they would then just copy the unions and try to outdo them in excess – like putting a refrigerator with beer and sandwiches in an executive's hotel room.

So GM had a reputation for arrogance spawned by the labor unions – that is where the refrigerator in the hotel room story got its traction. It was believed. That was a level of arrogance that was endemic at GM and perhaps still is.

What appears to have been missing at GM, and the other American auto companies as well, was management: a sense of trying to anticipate where the auto market was going, seeing what the emerging needs were, and pro-actively developing product solutions for those moves. Instead, GM just kept making the same old models until they couldn't sell them any more – there was no management.

The changing American automobile market imposed changes on GM rather than GM leading the evolution of the American auto experience. A good example is the emergence of seat belts. When seat belts were first proposed the Detroit automakers fought them, saying they would make the U.S. auto uncompetitive. The U.S. auto makers should have thought of seat belts first and proactively offered them without the need for Congressional legislation. But they didn't – and that makes the U.S. automakers a bad investment sector. On the other hand, foreign automakers may be a good investment, like Volkswagen, Mercedes-Benz and BMW.

As another example, take Boeing. They know at Boeing that the holy grail of airplane operation is speed, payload and fuel economy. So Boeing is on a never-ending quest to come out with a bigger, lighter, faster and more economical aircraft. And they do it about every 5 or 10 years. If Boeing had been run like GM, it too may have gone bankrupt. From an investor perspective, you can stay away from companies in decline by making sure the companies you are invested in are leading and not following the market.

For example, McDonald's is constantly changing its menu.

Procter & Gamble comes out with new products all the time. Jeff Bezos, at Amazon, is now talking about using drones to deliver Amazon packages. These are all un-GM-like characteristics.

But what is amazing about the GM story is that it remained in the two U.S. indices that we use to identify strong companies: The Dow Jones Industrial Average (the Dow 30) and the Standard & Poor (S&P 500). GM remained in these two indices right up to the point of declaring bankruptcy. This tells you that indices may not be a reliable way to find strong companies. You find strong companies by reputation; the reputation of GM was one of arrogance, and arrogance usually ends badly.

Back around 1955 I saw my first VW Beetle and could barely believe my eyes. Who would ever want this strange-looking car made in Germany with the engine in the rear instead of the front? At the time, in the U.S. auto market big was better and anybody who wanted a small car had no small American car options. Volkswagen saw that and soon there was a growing market for the VW Beetle in the U.S. Detroit didn't see it. Gradually, other cars made overseas began to enter the U.S. market, but the U.S. auto industry, headquartered in Detroit, just rolled over. This is a testament to the lack of leadership in the U.S. auto industry. The GM failure fit right in.

The attraction of the U.S. auto industry is its size. A car is one of the biggest expenses an American family undertakes, and every family has at least one car; many have two or more. So the auto market is huge.

But the labor unions have thoroughly penetrated the automakers, even pre-empting management initiatives with work rules. The management then loses its initiative; it becomes just a go-along get-along organization. And in a changing world, go-along get-along doesn't go very far. Companies that have a future are those that are leading innovators in their fields.

You can see the effect of the "Detroit labor-union way" on business. The Germans, the Japanese, the Koreans and the Swedes are having a field day over here selling all kinds of cars, and even those cars made in Detroit have much of their content coming in from overseas.

The lesson is, stay away from companies that can't change, no matter how big they are, and look for companies that create change, companies where the focus is on the brand and satisfying customers. Remember, a business is defined by customers, not products.

Iconic Companies

The way I pick stocks is to decide on what businesses I like and then find leading companies in those businesses. I also find companies by reputation. For example, many years ago I learned that, at that time anyway, recent college graduates could apply for an entry job at Procter & Gamble (P & G) and find themselves rotated throughout the company to learn how each department functioned. Later in their career, as they moved into management, they would know how each department contributed to the whole organization. This seemed to be a hallmark of a great company to me and primed me to be receptive to news about P&G.

So today, although I am exposed to news on many companies, not much of it registers with me unless it is news on companies I am interested in, like P&G. When I hear P&G mentioned, I immediately perk up and pay attention.

I have the same feelings about other companies, for example Royal Dutch Shell, the oil company, and Exxon-Mobil, another oil company. I also follow Johnson & Johnson; Nestle; Kellogg's; Cummins, a diesel engine manufacturer; ITW, an industrial conglomerate; Caterpillar; and Atlas-Copco, a Swedish manufacturer of construction equipment, just to name a few. I read a few years ago that Kellogg's was introducing Corn Flakes into India, changing the breakfast habits of about a billion people. This is the type of marketing initiative you are looking to invest in.

These are all iconic companies that have become part of the fabric of American life, so I can see on a day-to-day basis how my investment is doing without consulting the stock market. Some businesses I don't like are like the auto business because of the out-of-control union content. Auto workers earn a share of the American employment dollar that is out of proportion to their contribution.

How can this happen in a capitalist system? Unions. Unions demand and get wages and benefits not for the work they do, but by the "bargaining" they do: *"Give us what we want or we will strike!"* You will notice they don't want what is earned but what they can get through intimidation.

I also don't like airline stocks because there you do have competition, often brutal competition, but the business is a service business which may sacrifice service in the interests of financial viability. Anybody who flies today will tell you what an unhappy experience that is. There is just too much stress in the airline industry and you don't need it, there are better businesses.

I like some retailing stocks, like Walmart, because they are highly differentiated service businesses. There is a lot more difference between Walmart and K-Mart than there is between, for example, American Airlines and United Airlines. Walmart has built a global retailing powerhouse on the work of Sam Walton, who discovered that it is not the manufacturers who have customers but the stores selling the manufacturers' products who have the customers – and whoever has the customers makes the rules. Also, Walmart was a target for labor union organizing and in one case they just shut the store down. This lets you know management is doing what it is supposed to be doing – managing.

Up until the emergence of Sam Walton, manufacturers would dictate to the retailer what the program was: which products to offer to the public, where to place them in the store and what to charge for them. Sam Walton changed that. He said, in essence: *it is my store and my customers; I will decide what to sell where and at what price.* Today as a result of that, instead of Walmart people going to Cincinnati to plead for access to a new P&G product, P&G people go to Bentonville, Arkansas, to learn how they have to put identification on their packaging to comply with the Walmart inventory tracking system. This is the value of having customers, and a good lesson in investment: don't look at the companies and the products, look at the customers and what they are buying and why.

Where to Find Good Stocks

A good company is one that is focused not on the product of the day, but on the brand. A good example of a company responding to the constant challenge of change is General Electric. GE began as a light-bulb manufacturer but soon began to make anything connected to electricity, including inventing some products, like electric blankets. If you study the history of GE, you will realize that what is important at GE is not the products, but the brand. The brand is the focus as the company constantly re-invents itself to remain a strong business and a technology leader.

Many companies, like GE, have multiple products that are in various stages of their life cycles, and some companies are in multiple businesses with multiple products. For example, The Home Depot is in only one business – retailing. But The Home Depot constantly upgrades the mix of products they sell, so for them there is constant renewal.

General Electric is in many businesses: appliances, locomotives and aircraft engines to name three. At GE they maintain a portfolio of businesses that they are constantly evaluating, for growth, or for harvesting, or for selling off. High-growth, high-profit businesses are grown, or invested in. If a business has no future but is profitable, that business will be harvested, which is to say maintained but not grown. This is a business than spins off cash. Other businesses, that are declining and will ultimately require investment just to shut down, are sold off while they still have value.

Because you want to invest in companies that are innovative and focused on growing their brand, a good place to look for companies to invest in is to visit the Interbrand website – www.interbrand.com. Go to the Interbrand site and bring up the most recent report on global brand rankings. When I visited the site, the 100 top-ranked global brands in order of their rankings were:

1		2	Google	3	Coca-Cola	4	
5	Microsoft	6	GE	7	M	8	SAMSUNG
9	intel	10	TOYOTA	11	Mercedes-Benz	12	BMW
13	CISCO	14	Disney	15	hp	16	Gillette
17	LOUIS VUITTON	18	ORACLE	19	amazon	20	HONDA
21	H&M	22	pepsi	23	AMERICAN EXPRESS	24	Nike
25	SAP	26	IKEA	27	ups	28	ebay
29	Pampers	30	Kellogg's	31	Budweiser	32	HSBC
33	J.P.Morgan	34	VW	35	Canon	36	ZARA
37	NESCAFÉ	38	GUCCI	39	L'ORÉAL PARIS	40	PHILIPS
41	accenture	42	Ford	43	HYUNDAI	44	Goldman Sachs
45	SIEMENS	46	SONY	47	THOMSON REUTERS	48	citi
49	DANONE	50	Colgate	51	Audi	52	f
53	Heinz	54	HERMÈS PARIS	55	adidas	56	Nestlé
57	NOKIA	58	CATERPILLAR	59	AXA	60	Cartier
61	DELL	62	xerox	63	Allianz	64	PORSCHE
65	NISSAN	66	KFC	67	Nintendo	68	Panasonic
69	Sprite	70		71	Morgan Stanley	72	PRADA
73		74	VISA	75	TIFFANY & CO.	76	3M
77	BURBERRY	78	MTV	79	Adobe	80	JOHN DEERE

81	Johnson&Johnson	82		83	KIA	84	Santander
85	DURACELL	86		87	AVON	88	RALPH LAUREN
89	CHEVROLET	90	Kleenex	91		92	Heineken open your world
93	Corona Extra	94	Pizza Hut	95	SMIRNOFF	96	HARLEY DAVIDSON
97	MasterCard	98		99	MOËT & CHANDON	100	GAP

The methodology used by Interbrand is explained at their website:

> *"The brand must be truly global and needs to have successfully transcended geographic and cultural boundaries. It must have expanded across the established economic centers of the world, and be establishing a presence in the major markets of the future. In measurable terms, this requires that:*
>
> o *At least 30 percent of revenues must come from outside the brand's home region*
> o *It must have a presence in at least three major continents, as well as broad geographic coverage in emerging markets*
> o *There must be sufficient publicly available data on the brand's financial performance*
> o *Economic profit must be expected to be positive over the longer term, delivering a return above the brand's operating and financing costs*
> o *The brand must have a public profile and awareness above and beyond its own marketplace."*

Compare the above Interbrand rankings with the Dow 30 seen below. There are some obvious omissions, for example AT&T and Verizon, but these are excluded by

Interbrand because they are not global companies but operate in their home countries only. AT&T is on Interbrand's 100 Top American brands list. Walmart is excluded because it doesn't use the Walmart brand in all countries, but they are on the U.S. list and #1 on the top retailers list. Boeing also is on the U.S. list as a top brand.

The other obvious lapses are companies that are historically iconic companies but perhaps have not been doing too much brand building lately. I am referring to Alcoa,

Chevron, Dupont, Exxon-Mobil, United Technologies, Travelers and a few others. But the core activity of investment is investment and not company searches. All an investor needs is access to the Interbrand rankings.

Here are the Dow 30 with the 10 longest-serving constituents underlined:

COMPANY	SYMBOL	INDUSTRY	ADDED TO INDEX
3M	MMM	Conglomerate	1976
Alcoa	AA	Aluminum	1959
American Express	AXP	Financial	1982
AT&T	T	Telecom	1999
Bank of America	BAC	Banking	2008
Boeing	BA	Aerospace	1987
Caterpillar	CAT	Construction	1991
Chevron	CVX	Oil & Gas	2008
Cisco Systems	CSCO	IT	2009
Coca-Cola	KO	Beverages	1987
DuPont	DD	Chemicals	1935
Exxon-Mobil	XOM	Oil & Gas	1928
General Electric	GE	Conglomerate	1896
Hewlett-Packard	HPQ	Computers	1997
The Home Depot	HD	Retailing	1999

Intel	INTC	Semiconductors	1999
IBM	IBM	IT	1979
Johnson & Johnson	JNJ	Medical	1997
JP Morgan Chase	JPM	Banking	1991
McDonalds	MCD	Restaurant	1985
Merck	MRK	Pharma	1979
Microsoft	MSFT	Software	1999
Pfizer	PFE	Pharma	2004
Procter & Gamble	PG	Consumer	1932
Travelers	TRV	Insurance	2009
UnitedHealth Group	UNH	Health Care	2012
United Technologies	UTX	Conglomerate	1939
Verizon	VZ	Telecom	2004
Walmart	WMT	Retailing	1997
Walt Disney	DIS	Entertainment	1991

The Dow 30 is the Wall Street view of the Interbrand top global brands. The difference is that in the Dow 30 all you see are the stocks, whereas in the Interbrand listings you see companies dedicated to growing a brand. It is brand strength that makes strong and profitable companies, the ones that provide long-term investment returns.

I like 3M Company because it is broadly diversified internally and doesn't have any direct competitors, just competitors in their individual markets. I also read some years ago that at 3M Company, when employees get an idea for a new product, the company gives them the resources needed to develop the product; so what is important to this company is not its products but empowering people to find new solutions.

Caterpillar is another great company; it sells heavy construction equipment all over the world and has been in the news recently for not caving in to union action.

Management at Caterpillar has decided that they, rather than the union, will run the company. This is a good investment thesis –

management that manages.

Cisco is a company in a fast-changing, competitive market for IT solutions but has managed to stay ahead of the pack through it all. DuPont is another favorite of mine. This company has been a chemical powerhouse since the founding of our country, with the manufacture of gunpowder.

Exxon-Mobil and Royal Dutch Shell are the top dogs when it comes to oil exploration, refining and distribution. I always liked the Mobil *Speedpass*, the most sensible way to buy fuel for your car.

I have been an Intel fan ever since graduate school, where I read that Robert Noyce, one of the founders, soon after starting the company received a truck delivery of used desks for all the employees and took the most beat-up desk for himself. Obviously, here was a man who was more interested in getting a job done and inspiring others rather than furnishing his office.

There is another prophetic story about Noyce. While attending Grinnell College in Iowa, he and a friend stole a pig for a Hawaiian-style luau. They went and confessed to the aggrieved farmer and got into some trouble over it. But it does show the intrepid nature of the man. I presume Intel retains some of the Noyce character.

Johnson & Johnson is an iconic company whose brand is legendary on Band-Aids and baby shampoo, as well as many other standard drugstore products.

McDonald's has competition, but just enough competition to keep it an international icon – and have you ever had better fries? Also, McDonald's is in 119 countries the last time I looked. This is a business that isn't going away anytime soon and almost has a global monopoly. Additionally, every time I walk into a McDonald's, there is something new on the menu. This is a very innovative company.

Merck is in a tough business – pharmaceuticals. Companies spend a lot of money on research and development and if they come up with a breakthrough product, they only get 17 years patent protection on it, then anybody can copy and sell the formula as their own without the cost of the original research. So pharmaceutical companies have to keep the new product pipeline full of new promising compounds. Not many companies can do this, so pharmaceutical companies do occupy a place of great respect.

What got me interested in Merck was calling on their West Point, PA, facility as a sales engineer and seeing a horse in a corral right at the entrance. I asked the security guard what the horse was doing there. He told me that once a month, a Merck employee came out and took a syringe full of blood that was used to make a vaccine that Merck donated to the world to vaccinate against or cure some disease. I was very impressed and have followed Merck ever since.

Microsoft comes as close to any company, like McDonald's, to having a global monopoly. McDonald's has its monopoly by location, they are everywhere. Microsoft has its monopoly in the basic economic reality that people will always take the path of least resistance – that means using a Microsoft product instead of learning a new software program. I hate dealing with new software applications so I will buy a Microsoft product every time. I regularly read that this or that European country is levying fines against Microsoft for monopolizing some aspect of computer use. Well, I bet the people making those complaints are doing it in MS Word.

Procter & Gamble I have already talked about, and I will say unequivocally, P&G should be the first stock you buy.

Walmart I have already discussed as well, but I will add to it. I recently ordered two cables and a switch to share a printer between two computers. Soon after a box arrived; inside was a switch and one cable although the packing list listed two cables in the shipment.

I sent an email as directed at the Walmart online shopping site. The following morning I received a very apologetic message from Walmart stating that they were putting a cable in the mail that day. Soon a second box arrived with one cable in it. And soon after that came another apologetic email apologizing once again for the error and urging me to contact them again if I had any more problems.

I was a little surprised they didn't make more of a fuss about it since the packing list listed two cables on the original shipment. Of course, nothing could be proven either way and I guess they just figured that a cable is a small price to pay for keeping a customer satisfied. I had new respect for Walmart and new confidence in online ordering from Walmart.

Wall Street

As you wade into the world of stocks you will soon begin to notice this rushing sound that sounds far away, but the more you investigate stocks the louder this sound becomes. Finally, like opening a door to a cataclysm of some sort, the sound becomes deafening. What you are hearing is the torrent of information on every conceivable stock idea ever conceived by man being promoted as the single investment idea that, if acted upon, will propel you into the ranks of Midas, the legendary king who was able to turn anything into gold by merely touching it. Stop. If somebody you never met is telling you something, you must ask yourself – why? Is it to enrich the source, or the destination – the idea merchant, or you?

Since stock price is a function of demand, those owning the stock wish to see demand rise to lift their stock prices. That gives rise to broadcasting promising "reports" on the stock they already own. Multiply this by many thousands of stocks and you have that deafening roar of information.

Information that really does carry the promise of riches tends to be hoarded, and produces not a deafening roar but a vacant silence. You must, at the very start of your investment life, turn off the deafening roar and focus only on those stocks that are right out in front of you, those you know already, like those mentioned above: Intel, Microsoft, McDonald's, Johnson & Johnson.

When you invest in a company by buying common stock in the company, the demand and therefore the price of the stock will fluctuate depending on the relative attractiveness of the stock compared with alternative stock choices. Good news on a stock may lead to a fall rather than a rise in price because the news was not as good as expected.

For example, investors may be expecting the announcement of earnings of say $5 million, but instead learn that the earnings announcement is $4.3 million. There are other investment candidates that perhaps announced earnings of $5.75 million, an earnings surprise to the upside. In such a case, investors will abandon the first company's stock and move their money into the second company's stock. The change in demand will have the predictable impact on stock price: falling demand triggering sagging prices, and rising demand triggering a surge in stock price.

You might ask why the stock price doesn't go to zero as all investors would be abandoning the laggard in favor of the more promising company. Many investors view the earnings announcement as only an insignificant transient data point in an otherwise long history of success, and recognize that the rosier-looking company will soon enough be required to report its own shortfall in earning expectations.

This is the business cycle, and no company is immune. Sure enough, if you examine the stock market for any length of time, what you see is a rising and falling sea of stocks each responding to their own inevitable business cycles. Sometimes the business cycle is very unique to one company and at other times it is more generalized, affecting all companies. But what you can count on is that over time, all good companies thrive by constantly adapting to markets and being receptive to new and better ways to do things.

Change will be constant and on a day-to-day basis, not always up; but over time, strong companies succeed because they are stronger and have developed internal cultures devoted to beating the competition. And competition is really the driver. Look for companies that succeed in competitive markets.

If I had to guess at an investment landscape sculpted by investment success, I would imagine a bowl-shaped curve much like a negative quadratic equation resembling a bowl-like parabolic curve. The horizontal axis would be time spent on investment analysis. The vertical coordinate would be return.

So the high returns would be associated with doing little to no work at the extreme left, and at the far end, devoting all of your time to security analysis. Both positions do well. The folks in the middle, who may be called "dabblers"– they dabble at stocks – are mostly losers because they don't give it enough study to gain the requisite experience, yet don't want to give up, perhaps in a quixotic attempt at "getting lucky." There are too many greedy people to allow anybody to succeed on luck. There is just no other way to put it. See the graph below that charts the relationship of time spent and investment success.

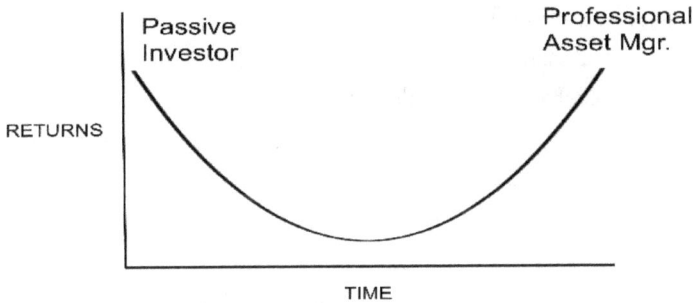

RETURNS

Passive Investor

Professional Asset Mgr.

TIME

As you can see from the chart, some professionals that spend their entire careers in security analysis may do well. But even many professionals don't do as well as passive investors in just the S&P 500 index. By far the best strategy for non-professionals is to pick out a few good stocks and then "set-it and forget-it."

There is another aspect to investing in stocks that the above illustration models: winners and losers. Investing in the stock-market is a zero-sum game, which means that when you add up all the wins and all the losses you get to zero, because the wins are exactly equal to the losses. In other words, you can't have winners without having losers: the money won is exactly equal to the money lost. Wins are just a transfer of money from somebody who bet wrong to somebody who bet right. So this is the everyday trading activity that produces winners because it also producers losers. And all of the wins are just on the value that is created up to that point in time. But value will continue to be created. So by just buying and holding a position in a company that is creating value and not trading out of that position (stock) is the certain way of winning. This is because those who bet right, only bet right some of the time. Those who buy and hold, passive investors, win all of the time. So getting back to the illustration above: the

Passive Investors are all the same people whereas the Professional Asset Manager population is constantly changing. So in the long-term curve, not the snapshot shown above, it is only the Passive Investors who win over the long term.

The stock market is like a drug for many and they just can't leave it alone. It is like gambling. There are people that just have to gamble, and the worst thing that can happen is an occasional win that only spurs more gambling. During one college summer I worked at a horse race track in a cashier's booth with six cashiers. Every one of those cashiers was a reformed gambler. And after I lost my shirt, I was too! In investment there are a lot of distractions. Better to pick out a few strong companies, invest in them monthly and put it on auto pilot.

The Life Cycle of a Business

All companies may be categorized by their position in the life cycle of companies. Companies start out as a "start-up," which for many is as far as they go, either going out of business or getting swallowed up by a competitor. Occasionally, start-up companies go mainstream and make it into the big time. McDonald's, Microsoft, and Johnson & Johnson, to name a few, were at one time start-up companies financed by family money.

Once in the big time, companies have to fight off competitors to thrive. This is the second stage. After fighting off competitors the third stage is reached, which is called the "Cash Cow" stage because money ordinarily used to start, defend or grow a business can now be spun off to investors who financed the company to begin with. Some businesses go on indefinitely, but the usual course is for companies to lose their edge as civilization advances, with customers tiring of the same old products and going out and buying the "latest & greatest."

If a company experiences this challenge, then they have to develop new products or eventually go out. Successful companies, the ones you want to invest in, are constantly reinventing themselves and not necessarily to catch up, but to get out ahead of the curve and create change for a new product they have developed. The great companies are the game changers. This is where GM failed.

Shown below is a popular 4-cell matrix that displays growth rate in the vertical coordinate and market share in the horizontal coordinate. The arrow shows the path companies take starting from the start-up "Question-Mark" stage.

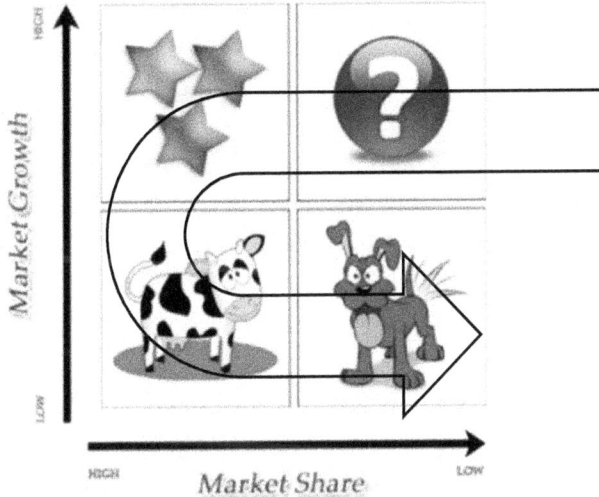

Companies generally start out trying to capture a new and fast-growing market, shown in the upper right corner as a question mark. If they succeed in beating out the competition, they become, appropriately enough, "Stars." As the competition falls off and the market stabilizes, money previously used to beat competitors now flows out to investors in the form of dividends, and the "Cash Cow" stage is reached. Over time, new replacement products or trend changes will erode the Cash Cow's market and a decline will begin, sometimes slowly but sometimes more quickly as the business enters the "Dog" stage before exiting entirely.

This matrix, attributed to the Boston Consulting Group, is designed to show that markets are not static but constantly changing, and that companies that act like GM are going to be investment losers. Most companies have a stable of products in different life cycle stages and they are constantly introducing new products and selling off declining products with a strategy of maximizing the value of their brand. Every time a product reaches market success, the brand is enhanced.

Many investors give very high priority to dividends in their stock selection and in retirement live mainly on the dividends. Not all stocks pay dividends since they are the result of cash not needed to grow the business. So dividends come from mature businesses or mature companies with a substantial portion of their products or businesses in the "Cash Cow" stage. In the U.S. these companies are listed on the New York Stock Exchange, NYSE, sometimes called "The Big Board" because of its imposing size compared to other stock exchanges.

Both The Home Depot and GE have evolved to a stage where they don't have serious challenges to their supremacy in their business sectors, so they can afford to spin off cash to investors while also growing new businesses. If you buy The Home Depot (HD) or GE (GE) stock, you are an investor and will realize that cash spin-off as quarterly dividend distributions to investors. Currently HD is paying 2%, or more correctly has an annual dividend yield on today's stock price of 2%. GE has a current yield of 3.20%.

Value and Growth Companies

NYSE-listed companies tend to be large and are therefore slower-growing because it is difficult to grow a number that is already huge. These companies are sometimes called *Value* companies because they are profitable, pay dividends and are generally pretty secure from any major competitive challenge, but mostly because they trade at lower earnings multiples. This is not to say that successful companies must be large, there are many very successful smaller companies.

There are also companies in faster-growing businesses that need their cash to maintain and grow the business to keep up with the markets they are in. These are called *Growth* companies and they do not pay dividends as a rule. These companies usually trade at higher earnings multiples and are listed at the NASDAQ exchange, whose non-abbreviated name is National Association of Securities Dealers Automated Quotations.

A logical question is why would investors prefer "Growth" companies that don't pay dividends over "Value" companies that do pay dividends? The answer is Capital Gains. When an investor purchases a stock and then sees the price of the stock rise, the investor may then count on realizing capital gains over time. Companies grow at different rates; investors in "Growth" companies are likely to realize faster growth rates and greater capital gains. But investors in "Value" companies will realize the value of their holding in a combination of dividends and capital gains. The gains from "Value" stocks may be the same as from "Growth" stocks, just comprised of less capital gain and more dividend distribution.

Also, "Growth" companies are on their way to becoming "Value" companies, they just haven't beaten out the competitors soundly enough to redirect research and marketing money to stockholders in the form of dividends – that will come later. This makes "Growth" company investing more of a challenge because they all will not succeed. "Value" company investing puts you into a slower-moving world that is not so vulnerable to competitive challenges.

Earnings Multiples or P/E Ratio

The total capitalization of a company may be calculated by adding up the number of shares that have been distributed to the public and then multiplying that number by the share price. The result is *capitalization*. There are large capitalization companies, sometimes called "Large- Cap." Then there are "Mid-Cap," "Small-Cap," "Micro-Cap," and "Nano-Cap" companies. So in addition to segmenting companies by "Value" and "Growth," companies may be segmented by capitalization size.

The total capitalization of a company tells you, more or less, what a company is worth today. If you wanted to own that company, you wouldn't need to wonder how much it would take to buy it, you would just calculate the total capitalization and that is what the company costs to buy – today. Of course, once you owned the company, you would want to know what it is really worth; this would be calculated from earnings, how much is the company making.

Slow-growing companies are capitalized at about twelve times annual earnings, or have a price-earnings (P/E) ratio of 12.

Theoretically, after 12 years the buyer will be completely repaid for his purchase. Everything after that is profit. In truth, the buyer will be repaid ahead of 12 years because the company is growing and may be expected to double in earnings over a 12-year period. But an earnings multiple of 12 is the default price of slower-growing companies.

Faster-growing companies trade at higher earnings multiples or a higher P/E. A tech company in a fast-growing business might be selling at a P/E of 50. This indicates the company is in an earlier life-cycle stage and must use earnings to invest in product development and marketing to remain viable. The allure in this company is that it may succeed in beating out its competitors and the stock price may rise dramatically as the company comes to dominate its market. This is a case where the company gradually acquires pricing power and becomes very profitable, eventually rewarding stockholders with dividend distributions; but in the meantime, it rewards stockholders with dramatic capital gains in the form of dramatic stock price appreciation.

While "Value" stock investing may be safer, "Growth" stock investing may be more profitable, so a good strategy might be to own a few "Growth" stocks in a mostly "Value" stock portfolio.

Portfolio Design

Some investors create a portfolio of stocks which they populate with both "Value" and "Growth" stocks. In fact, a well-diversified portfolio will contain not only diversification by Value and Growth, but also by capitalization size.

Companies are ranked by size by capitalization into generally three ranks: Large Cap, Mid Cap and Small Cap. Capitalization is calculated by multiplying the number of shares of stock held by investors by their current market price. For example, GE has a market capitalization of about $250 billion and is currently trading at about $25/share. So there are about 10 billion shares outstanding.

One of my favorites stocks is Cummins, a diesel engine manufacturer. Cummins is currently trading at about $130/share and has a capitalization of about $24 billion with about 185,000 shares outstanding. GE has a current dividend yield of 3.20% while Cummins has a current dividend yield of 1.90%. But Cummins has a dividend payout ratio of about 27% while GE has a payout ratio of 51%. The payout ratio is the proportion of profits directed to dividend distribution.

Payout decisions are made by the Board of Directors and CEO based on forecast cash requirements and will change with changing business conditions. But these variations between companies result in varying responses to the business cycle, so that creating a diversified portfolio not only reduces volatility, but gives the portfolio characteristics that allow it to better negotiate changing economic conditions. Remember, you never know where the economy is going, so it is better to try to prepare for all possible outcomes.

GE is in many businesses and so has greater stability in changing economic cycles. Cummins makes mainly diesel engines and engine components, so is much more vulnerable to business-cycle downturns. Putting both GE and Cummins into a portfolio provides the opportunity for growth with the stabilizing effect of diversity, but they are both heavily industrial and will not ride out a market downturn like a food company for example, like Kellogg's. So adding Kellogg's to your portfolio of GE and Cummins would be a good diversifying component.

Volatility

As has been illustrated, the stock market reacts almost instantly to news with a bipolar personality that reels in would-be exploiters to either buy in just ahead of the news or anticipate the news and buy in early. If the information is not acquired from those inside the corporation being targeted for investment, it is thought to be legal and therefore actionable by investors. But in many cases, the stock price behavior does not follow script and those "in the know" take on losses rather than gains. The only reliable information is inside information, and it is illegal to trade on that information.

The global stock market contains the total global capitalization of all public companies, so it is a huge amount of money and attracts a commensurate amount of global study by a very large and diverse population, all focused on the same thing – converting their knowledge into money. This makes the market very efficient, in that any information at all that is actionable very quickly gets converted into action, and the stock price moves up or down as a result.

Inside information often is pent-up information that has not even been partially made public and is therefore much more likely to have a more predictable and larger effect on stock price, up or down. Since the predictability and scale of the information is significant, the rule is that it must be distributed to the public in such a way that allows the broader market to get the information simultaneously. Typically the information is communicated in a news release to the media. Then the very predictable trading will occur, propelling stock price in the expected direction in the scale proportional to its impact on future earnings.

Records are kept of all trades, and the agency empowered to police the stock market and insider trading will examine trading records for any unusual activity, like the elderly grandmother in Iowa buying a gazillion shares ahead of some public announcement. If grandma has a track record of making such insightful buys at a similar scale, she will be left alone. But if grandma is, like many grandmas, more interested in collecting her dividend checks, she will be asked what prompted her to make such a large uncharacteristic investment.

Inevitably it will be found that she has a grandson, or other youthful relative, with some connection to an individual employed at a company that got the inside information and thought that sharing the wealth with a friend with a grandmother in Iowa would be a fool-proof way to cash in. The trade will be "busted", which is to say unwound, and the insider will be prosecuted.

Nevertheless, much investment and one may argue almost all investment, and indeed, market price behavior as a whole, is largely driven by a subset of investors seeking to profit from what is felt to be information that is not yet broadly available, but imminently will be. These investors drive price behavior. Price behavior is very reliable and it has always been so – it is reliably erratic. Think bipolar person cycling between mania and deep depression throughout the day, from market open to market close. This is the market – total freedom, total paranoia.

As you might imagine, the market exhibits great volatility cycling between euphoria and fear but not equally across all issues – some stocks will really not react all that much while other stocks will gyrate wildly on a procession of news both good and bad. Accordingly, stocks exhibit volatile price behavior but in an array from very volatile to not very volatile at all.

Beta, a Measure of Volatility

In the study of physics, water was selected as a ubiquitous and bland material denoting a neutral state and therefore arbitrarily assigned a specific gravity of 1. All other compounds have their specific gravity determined by a comparison to the density of water. In investment, the S&P 500 has been denoted as having a "specific gravity" of 1, with the term being attached to it of *beta*, the second letter of the Greek alphabet.

Perhaps beta was selected because in science a beta version is the latest version and may represent a changed state. In any case, all stocks may have their volatility measured and compared to the volatility of the S&P 500 and may then be assigned a beta volatility value.

Stocks that exhibit less volatility than the S&P 500 will be denoted by values less than 1, for example .5 beta for a stock that moves up and down at half the rate of the S&P 500. This might be a very slow-changing but successful company like a public power generation utility that will see its business cycle quite muted since electric power demand is pretty steady regardless of economic conditions.

Companies that are in the early stages of their development with frequent new product announcements are likely to have a beta of 2 or more, being quite bipolar in their stock price behavior. Then there are counter-cyclical companies that may move opposite to the S&P 500, for example a food company that sees sales rise in hard times. If the stock price behavior is equal to but opposite to the S&P 500, then it might have a beta of -1. More muted but opposite stock price movement would earn the stock a beta of -.5.

In any case, beta values are routinely published along with other stock market metrics like P/E, dividend yield, etc., to help investors make stock selections. But be careful: like other stock market characteristics, business is a world that creates change and it is change that people are investing in. The very metrics people are basing their investment decisions on are also constantly changing and maybe even calling into question their assumptions in making the investment in the first place – be careful of stock market metrics.

Volatility is typically reviled by the market because it means investments are going down as well as up, in a bipolar world that generally trends up with the value creation that business continually builds. But value creation comes in spurts, not the neat smooth upwardly-trending line investors yearn for. The investor's world is a bipolar one and there will be downs as well as ups.

But for the investor choosing regularized investments, like monthly purchases of a target stock, described later as dollar-cost averaging, the dips are opportunities to buy favored stocks at lower prices; for those investors, volatility takes on a whole new meaning.

Investing in Companies

The stock market exists to finance industry, and the success of the American economy and American industry is a testament to the successful functioning of the American stock market, made up of multiple stock exchanges of which the NYSE and NASDAQ are only two.

Investors will put money into stocks only if they can get their money back out if they need to. This is called *liquidity*, the power to quickly convert stock to cash.

Without liquidity investment would be discouraged, and we could not have the wealthy nation that we do that provides jobs, products and infrastructure for us to both get to our jobs and enjoy the products that we make. Liquidity is crucial.

When you buy stock, you are allowing an earlier investor to

reclaim his cash for some other purpose, maybe to buy a different stock. But the purchase of the stock is what keeps companies well financed so that they can pursue their mission.

A stockholder is also a stakeholder in the fortunes of the corporation. Those fortunes are determined by the effectiveness of company management, the nature of the competitive market they operate in and an American infrastructure that supports the demand for and use of the company's products. So while the stock certificate is just a piece of paper denoting ownership, it represents real economic activity that benefits everybody.

When you invest in company stock, go to the company's website and learn what it is they do. It is in understanding what you are financing with your stock purchases, your investing, that much of the psychic reward comes from and makes you a better and wiser investor.

Sometimes investors get so caught up in the stock market action that they lose sight of the fact that the stock market is a proxy for the real market, where people go to work every day to create the products that then compete in a real market to satisfy everyday consumer needs.

Hopefully this book will propel you in the direction of knowing what companies you are invested in and why. Some companies are in better businesses and have better management; this is not information you will glean from looking at a ticker symbol or a stock quote.

If you want to learn more about a company you can write to the Investor Relations department and request an annual report. They will be delighted to send you one, or you may download it from their website.

Annual reports are, first of all, designed to sell, so be careful of just accepting everything you read. But the report will tell you what businesses the company is in, and the letter from the CEO will talk about what the overall strategy is and how the company is utilizing its assets and its brand to maximize value for shareholders.

Chapter 5

Corporate Governance

MOST COMPANIES IN THE S&P 500 are what are called "C" corporations, which is the standard corporate legal model for most companies. This may come as a surprise – that companies are bound by a legal framework – but unless there are legal constraints and remedies, some people might not be all that cooperative and might not work for the overall good, being more concerned with their individual good.

The founding of our country was done by legal corporate structure. The Jamestown settlement in 1607 in Virginia was the first North American corporate venture; that didn't do so well but the second corporate venture, the Plymouth Colony in 1620, did very well and ramped up North American settlement by Europeans.

The Virginia Company

The original Plymouth settlers were obligated, by law, to repay the cost of their voyage to the Virginia Company by shipping back timber, furs, dried cod and anything else of value that they found in their area of settlement. The expectation was that the Plymouth colony would send back enough goods to make the original voyage a profitable one, repaying original investors with a profit.

The organizers of the Virginia Company were entrepreneurs who no doubt were very much aware of the enrichment Spain had obtained from bringing gold and silver back from their colonies in the New World, repaying the original investment many times over. There had been earlier voyages of exploration to North America but no gold or silver was ever found, so the Virginia Company was pretty much focused on timber, furs and dried cod that had all found a market in England.

The challenge the Virginia Company founders had was attracting investment to finance voyages; for that they had English law that made provision for "chartered" for-profit companies that would be protected by the Crown. Theoretically, if the Plymouth colony settlers did not repay the Virginia Company, the English Navy would be sent to Plymouth to round up and return the settlers to England for court action and, presumably, long jail sentences. In any case, this didn't happen. The Plymouth colony was very profitable and soon prompted the proliferation of new colonies, all with royal charters defining their geography, legal construction and objective.

It is worthwhile making a detour into early colonial economic history to make an important point. The first Plymouth pilgrim settlers were, apparently, not very good farmers from Scrooby, England, and opted to face living in the wilderness to avoid prosecution that would carry a death sentence (otherwise it is very difficult to get people to leave their comfortable beds for life in the wilderness). The Crown owned all the land and distributed it by "grant." So the sponsors of the Mayflower voyage may have had a land grant from the king; it was within their power to distribute this land to the settlers.

Initially, all the settlers got a plot of land to build a house and shared a common pasture for their animals, which evolved into the town green in many New England towns. The limitation was not land, but clearing the land to make it suitable for farming and pasture. In general, a family got as much land as they could clear and then had ownership of that land, on which they would literally grow their estate.

Life was tough back then, but don't confuse tough with poverty. Land is wealth. Many of these families accumulated and cleared land and became wealthy from this work, earning revenue from crops and animal husbandry and building up substantial estates. The Pilgrims wound up wealthy while their relatives back in Scrooby remained poor, not having the same ready access to land. Giving up their comfortable beds to go live in the wilderness paid off.

Today, we are no longer Pilgrims but are more like the poor relatives back in Scrooby, scratching out a living in a landless world. The land has always been a "factor of production;" today it is the businesses that occupy the land that hold opportunity. That opportunity is obtained not by trying to farm what open land there is, but by farming the occupied land by acquiring the common stock in the companies occupying the land and making profit in a variety of businesses.

In 1620, the road to success was successful farming, while today the road to success is successful investment. But here is the key concept: the Pilgrims understood that their survival depended upon their ability to farm. Today, many people don't understand that investment in the companies occupying the land is just as much a requirement for living as farming was to the Pilgrims.

Investment in the common stock of the world's great corporations isn't an optional exercise for a small subset of the population born to it; it is an absolute requirement for everybody, particularly the poorer members of our society who have not been "born" to wealth. Parents do not understand the necessity of teaching their children about the need to invest in the common stock of the world's great corporations. It is the principal way wealth is built. The other way wealth is built is also investment, but in real estate.

There is one other lesson from colonial America. Englishmen visiting the American colonies were always amazed at the wealth they encountered in what they believed was a backward culture living in the wilderness. The origin of the wealth was living in an economy that was growing rapidly, due to a rapidly-swelling population producing a rapidly-growing market that created unparalleled opportunity for all participants. Farmers, candle makers, tavern keepers, carpenters, shipbuilders and all tradesmen could look forward to thriving growing businesses, all trying to serve a rapidly growing population. Today, with a much slower-growing population, that same level of opportunity that greeted those early settlers is gone.

The objective then, as it is now, was profit. A company has a legal requirement to make profit. If a company is not profitable, it has no reason for existing and is disbanded. But what all companies must do, as the Virginia Company did, is aggregate investment from many people to assemble a large enough capital base to finance whatever the company is going to do to make a profit. Very few individuals have the wealth individually to finance the start-up of a corporation and so must turn to financing from multiple outsiders.

How Companies are Formed

Many corporate start-ups are family affairs where inventors or entrepreneurs turn to family to finance a venture. At some point a new idea is established as a product, and it becomes clear to outsiders that there is an opportunity to provide investment at an early stage of a product life cycle and reasonably expect a dramatic return in profit. The early family investors are usually inspired by their knowledge of their relative as perhaps "creative" and "industrious," so they put in a modest part of their savings. Outsiders are not so easily inspired; they have to see some proof that a product has a market that only needs investment to make it succeed. Only then will outsiders gain enough inspiration to invest.

As soon as entrepreneurs turn to the public for investment, government steps in, creating a whole host of legal structures that must be satisfied before a public offering may be made. This goes back in history to primarily Dutch and English origins of stopping fraudulent schemes that often grew out of control, like fires that left a wake of destruction in their paths.

One such scheme that created total chaos in London was the South Sea subscription that later became known as the South Sea Bubble. The English government sold a large quantity of sovereign bonds to a developer, who paid for them by selling shares in the South Sea venture. Londoners were very familiar with the wealth the Spanish brought home from their "South Sea" ventures. They expected their English counterparts could do the same thing and bought up the shares with great energy. Even one of the most intelligent of Londoners, the famous physicist Sir Isaac Newton, was inspired to buy shares. But when it became apparent that the venture was overvalued, investors headed for the exits *en masse*. Of course, most lost all of their savings, including Newton.

Early on, from the South Sea Bubble and other busts, it was noted that the public is not capable of acting responsibly when promised a very profitable return on any investment idea that sounds good. And so governments stepped in to make order, passing laws on what needed to be in place before a public offering could be made. These laws have evolved over the years, but are all intended to protect the interests of unsuspecting investors lured by unsubstantiated promises of riches.

In the United States, all public offerings must be made with a prospectus that provides detail on how much is to be raised, how it will be invested, how repayment will be made and who is responsible. The first public that must be satisfied, however, is the investment bank that will prepare the offering documents. If they don't see a viable business, the project won't go anywhere.

Then the exchange on which the new company will be listed will have to agree to list the stock offering. So, since the public is in no position to even judge the contents of a prospectus, the first publics that must be reassured are the enabling merchant bank and the listing exchange. The listing exchange, for example NYSE (New York Stock Exchange), must see in the prospectus a viable business and sufficient interest in the issue to prompt a liquid market. If it is perceived that early investors cannot easily cash out due to the absence of willing new buyers, then the issue will not be listed and the ability of the venture to raise public capital will be severely curtailed.

Initial Public Offering - IPO

Most issues that are listed by the various stock exchanges are for companies that have products that have gone mainstream and are doing a robust business already, all financed by family members and close business associates. The purpose of the offering, IPO (Initial Public Offering), is to ramp up the financing to take the product to the next level, which may be general domestic public use or into general global use, and to pay off the start-up investors.

When I was a stock broker, I was in conversation with a young woman who had recently graduated from college and was working at an entry-level job for a prominent company at its Manhattan headquarters. She had an impressive amount of money – I am recalling an amount around $700,000.

She described a cousin starting a business that had, at that time, evolved into a well-known but not large public company. The cousin had used close family money to get the business started but soon needed more than the immediate family could supply. He went to his wealthy grandmother, who had a very novel way to finance her grandson. The grandmother contacted all of her children and grandchildren and required them to contribute to the family venture, but if it went bust, she would personally repay them. If the business succeeded the relatives could keep their winnings. It worked. The family contributed heavily and eventually the venture went public in an IPO. A portion of the proceeds of the IPO went to repay the original family investors; this young woman wound up with her share being around $700,000.

Before the IPO stage, investors can be pretty well assured that their investments are being used in the most responsible way and will have some record of how many private shares they own. It may also be that pre-IPO capital is not well spent – I am sure there are cases where entrepreneurs make off with the family money and are not heard from again for a very long time. But once the venture goes IPO, which means to the unsuspecting public, then assets are not so casually accounted for and a number of accounting procedures and fraud-defeating procedures come into play.

In order to access the public capital markets, a pre-IPO company engages an investment banking firm, sometimes called a merchant banking firm. The investment banking firm then decides how attractive the IPO will be. If they feel it is a winner, they may provide the capital directly to the pre-IPO company by buying all the shares. Once the shares are owned by the investment banking firm, they are offered to the public at an opening price that is a spread over what was paid for the shares. If the firm bought the shares for $15 it might offer them to the public at, say $18 per share, and pocket the spread of $3 per share, which for 2,000,000 shares might be $6 million. A very nice payday unless the shares don't sell, and the investment bank winds up owning the company.

If the investment bank thinks such a thing is even remotely possible, it will sell the shares to the public on a "best efforts" basis. In this case, the shares are not bought by the investment bank, they just take a commission on all sales. If the shares don't sell under the 'best-efforts" basis, the investment bank still loses money but a much smaller amount.

The loss stems from the very capital-intensive work involved in taking a company to the public. Accountants must be engaged to thoroughly audit company results, allowing them to fully disclose operating costs and profit so that the public may be fully informed if they read the offering prospectus. The prospectus will also contain a description of the business and list threats to the business in the form of competition and underlying market conditions that may pose a challenge to company prospects.

Attorneys are also engaged to make sure the prospectus complies with all disclosure requirements, to account for share ownership and to set up the legal documents so that investors and the public are aware of the limited liability of the corporation. For example, the corporation is a separate person and investors are only liable up to the value of their shares. If the company harms somebody and that person sues, the most that can be recovered is the value of the corporation, which is all assets including all outstanding stock. That is it – no more. Investors cannot lose their personal assets from corporate ownership in a corporation that becomes the target of a suit.

Protecting the Shareholder

Once the public is protected from fraudulent public offering schemes like the South Sea venture, there is the question of protecting the investor in a legitimate corporate enterprise. The problem arises because the public is in no way capable of offering value to the enterprise they are invested in beyond providing their money. Who is going to run the company and look after investor interests? After all, the company exists to make a profit, and whose profit is it but the investors'? But if the investors are not involved on a day-to-day basis, who is going to manage the company and their investments? For this there is corporate governance law.

In the United States, all corporate governance law is state law, so there are 50 models of corporate governance, each defined by what state a company is incorporated in. The only federal law touching on this subject is the federal law that a public corporation may establish headquarters and incorporate in any state of their choosing, without regard to its actual corporate footprint. For example, the early history of JC Penney stores began in Montana, but to be closer to the capital markets, the company at some point chose to be headquartered in New York City and perhaps incorporated in Delaware.

Today, most companies are incorporated in the state of Delaware because Delaware has the most liberal laws restraining corporate boards of directors – and it is the boards of directors that choose where the company will be incorporated.

If this makes you cynical about corporate governance, you should be. Recent evidence seems to point to competition among boards, resulting in outsize pay for CEOs they are supposed to be providing investor oversight on. It seems each board wants to work with the highest-paid CEO in the industry, so they bump up the pay package of "their" CEO. This is how investor's interests are being represented in the real world. While the board works on behalf of the investors in theory, in practice they work on behalf of their own interests and the interests of the CEOs that flatter them or otherwise cater to their egos and wallets. This may be cynical, but it is the way it is in the USA.

This phenomenon is called "capture," where those doing the oversight are captured by those being overseen. It is frequently the case in board oversight of C- corporations and government oversight of business sectors they are supposed to be monitoring. This was anticipated as far back as the 18th century by Adam Smith, who wrote:

> [Investors] *"...seldom pretend to understand anything of the business of the company.....and [Directors] being managers of other people's money rather than their own, it cannot well be expected that they should watch over it with the same anxious vigilance with which the partners in a private co-partnery frequently watch over their own."*

However, each company is different. There is a tendency among investors to lump all corporate culture into one paradigm, but this would be an error. Each company has a distinct culture, and what may pass as good governance in one company may very well be rejected out-of-hand in another company. Pay attention to corporate culture. But it may be useful to look at the origin and rationale for boards in the first place.

The term "board" comes from an actual board. It was felt that members selected to represent interests of investors might begin to interfere unnecessarily in the running of a company; to head this off, members would not meet at a table with comfortable chairs that might invite prolonged meetings. Rather, a board was placed across two sawhorses, and investor representatives sat on stools when they met periodically to consider if corporate actions were carried out for the benefit of investors. Obviously, the furniture was very uncomfortable, prompting short meetings.

Such a group would need a leader to call meetings; that individual would have to be more engaged. Consequently, he or she got a chair rather than a stool, hence the term "Chairman."

So from this beginning we have today "Boards of Directors"

chaired by a "Chairman of the Board." Unfortunately, the furniture has been changed in that sawhorses and a board are no longer used, that I know of, and boards have largely lost their way and don't function in an oversight role at many companies.

In Delaware, as in all of the U.S., what is regarded as corporation law is two sets of laws: Articles of Incorporation, regulating external relationships; and Articles of Association, regulating internal relationships.

External issues are what product or service the corporation provides and the capitalization of the enterprise by outside stockholders. Internal issues are those affecting governance, such as procedures for board meetings.

The most important rules are those defining the relationship between the board of directors and the owners (shareholders). The core concept is that the board of directors has a right to manage the corporation for the benefit of the owners. Regulation of the board is contained in the Articles of Association and states specifically the number of "directors" (or "governors," "regents," "trustees," etc.), how they are chosen and when they are to meet.

The SEC & NYSE

I must acknowledge at the outset that I am cynical about U.S. corporate governance practices and hold up Germany as a model of rectitude for the same. As a matter of fact, much of the material for this section on German corporate governance came from a website of a German company, SGL Group of Wiesbaden, a company in the carbon processing business with a global footprint. At the same time, with obvious holes in corporate governance, American companies go around the world posing as the paragons of corporate virtue. To give a flavor, let me cite one example.

Enron was an energy company based in Houston that at one time boasted strict corporate governance and one of the longest-running records on distributing dividends. I know this because as a sales engineer I used to call on Enron and was advised on more than one occasion to buy Enron stock by some long-standing Enron engineers.

So Enron was on my radar.

Enter Ken Lay, who became Enron's Chairman & CEO and who had ideas of putting the Enron business on steroids. Ken hired a number of prominent graduates of fancy schools and gave them *carte blanche* to grow the business. One of these new hires conceived of the idea of offloading corporate acquisition costs – debt – onto off-balance-sheet entities that he invented for the purpose. In other words, these were other wholly-owned business entities, but their financial reports did not have to be included in the holding company report. The result was a balance sheet that showed a lot of growth with newly acquired entities but no debt associated with these acquisitions, since the debt followed the entities. This would be like you getting a loan for a car from an auto dealer but reporting the debt as dealer debt rather than your debt. This frees you up to get another auto loan, since according to your financials you have no prior auto debt.

Soon the market, observing this wonderful new growth without debt, bid up the stock into the stratosphere. Ken was told that the new stock valuations were achieved by the absence of full disclosure, and thinking that his personal shares would collapse in value, began importuning employees of Enron to buy Enron shares, which would be Ken's shares, the ones he would be selling. The inevitable crash came; however, the only sour note he received from the NYSE was that the loss of trading volume would force them to de-list Enron shares from the NYSE exchange.

Now, a similar listing tale with a different ending: Daimler-Benz, a German manufacturer of the highly coveted Mercedes-Benz automobile, wished to be listed on the Big Board, the NYSE. Accordingly, Daimler supplied the SEC and NYSE with accounting reports and other documents supporting their strict attention to accounting standards and sufficient interest in the issue to prompt brisk trading that would be well above NYSE thresholds. The NYSE examined the submission but found a problem with it, denying Daimler access to the U.S. capital markets. Daimler, as an accounting policy, underreported cash on hand and perhaps other assets. *"No good"* said the SEC or NYSE – it didn't meet American standards for "full-disclosure." Full disclosure? What about Enron? Enron failed to report debt but the listing was removed over trading volume, not disclosure. Daimler was not listed over disclosure meant to protect investors.

The failure at Enron to divulge all liabilities led to overly optimistic assessments of the Enron business, essentially defrauding investors. Underreporting assets is not a fraud in that it leads to a lower rather than a higher valuation of an asset. Daimler was just being very conservative in their estimation of enterprise worth. Investors in Daimler would not have been defrauded but rather more protected by the lack of disclosure. This is an example of why the American regulatory authorities over market operations are not to be entirely relied upon. This falls under the general heading of government agencies being "captured" by the organizations they are supposed to be regulating. This is an old and well-identified problem – what starts out as an "arm's length" relationship soon turns to capture, and the government agency is working for the entities it is regulating rather than working for the public.

American Depositary Receipts (ADRs)

Prominent foreign companies routinely have their shares traded in their home country, but offering the shares globally might increase demand for the shares and drive up the price accordingly. Higher-priced shares are advantageous to the company in offering an additional channel to raise money – issue more and more expensive shares. Accordingly, a number of German companies sought listing on U.S. exchanges to broaden access to their shares.

After the Enron collapse (described further on), the U.S. Congress passed a number of laws mandating rules designed to head off another Enron. These rules became so burdensome for companies to comply with that many German companies left the NYSE and NASDAQ markets, but are still traded in the U.S. as ADRs, American Depositary Receipts.

ADRs are issues of stock derived by holding foreign stock and re-issuing it in U.S. dollar-denominated "receipts." The stock is then mainly traded in the home market (Germany) and the OTC (Over the Counter) market. ADRs come in various levels of "sponsorship," or proximity to a sponsoring organization. The highest level of ADRs are sponsored ADRs and the lowest level are unsponsored ADRs. For more information point your browser to the OTC markets website. In any case, ADRs offer a way to hold shares in German companies and companies in other countries, denominated in U.S. dollars and in all other respects behaving like the source security, a share of German common stock including receipt of all dividends.

Investors vs. CEOs

A central issue with American corporate governance has to do with representing stockholder interests. This is typically the job of Chairman of the Board and board members. The Chairman is charged with heading up a board of directors to provide oversight on corporate management, headed up by the CEO (Chief Executive Officer). So these are two very powerful positions in a corporation but with somewhat conflicting interests. Both the stockholders and CEO want their company to succeed, but there will be competing claims to corporate profits. The shareholders will want profits directed toward Retained Earnings and Dividends. The CEO will want a larger proportion directed to his pay envelope. This is something that needs to be negotiated between the Board and the CEO.

In many U.S. companies, the position of Chairman of the Board and CEO are combined. When it comes to distributing earnings, how can the CEO represent the interests of the shareholders? The CEO may feel constrained to continue declaring, say a 5% dividend, but this is not synonymous with representing shareholders.

My own feelings are that CEO pay negotiations are pretty light and mostly go in favor of the CEO. The result, of course, is outsize pay packages for CEOs even when they stumble. And like labor unions, the highest pay package becomes the new norm regardless of the amount of distortion. For example, a recent New York Times editorial cited CEO pay rising from 30 times that of the lower paid workers in a company to, more recently, 270 times lower paid workers' wages since the 1960s.

The Meaning of "Rents"

When you collect a rent, you are collecting a cash stream that locks in a profit and a certainty of collection. That is what rent means. Economists use the term *rent* to mean a certain and profitable collection of revenue. In free markets, extraordinary profits or "rents" are squeezed out by competitors, so the only profit left is what competitors regard as too small to bother with, which is "ordinary profit." The loss of extraordinary profit that attends new businesses then causes entrepreneurs to seek new ways to make extraordinary profit – this is what drives economic activity that benefits society as a whole.

The central concept of a market is that there will be more sellers than buyers, so the competition among sellers for the few buyers will drive down price and profit to a level that will barely support the sellers. Some sellers will find the profit too thin and will exit the market and attempt a new venture which will, for a while, provide richer profits. Eventually, the richer venue attracts more competitors and the business is ruined like the last business, so new businesses must be started in search of new profits. It is in this never-ending quest for extraordinary profit that produces economic activity that benefits all of society.

Some areas of new company activity are so expensive that no entrepreneur would bother with it, denying society the good that such an enterprise might contribute to the general welfare, such as development of medicines. To plug that societal hole, government steps in to issue patents for developments that protect the extraordinary profits of entrepreneurs for a period of years, at one time 17 years. So for 17 years, entrepreneurs can be rent collectors, but at patent expiration competitors come in and spoil the fun. Time for a new development and a new patent. But in this way great new developments are created for the public.

Monopolies

There are some sectors of the economy that have patent-like

protections that never expire; economists refer to these activities as "rent" collection. An example of rents is labor unions where, for example, a carpenter for Carnegie Hall will be compensated many times the actual market value for his services. When his outrageous demands are questioned, he may threaten to shut down a performance for which his contribution is a little carpentry, work that could be performed by any one of 10,000 area carpenters for little more than the price of a few tickets. That is rent.

Another example of rent, but of legitimate rent, is unprotected monopolies. Monopolies are obtained when all competing sellers exit the market, usually because they are unable to compete on quality or cost or any number of other dimensions. One example is Microsoft. Microsoft commands a monopoly because the product is, first of all, ubiquitous – nobody can survive very long without Microsoft software. The second enabling component of Microsoft's monopoly is inertia: who would want to take the time to learn a new competing software program? What would be the advantage? And if there is room for improvement in a Microsoft product, Microsoft will be the first to fix that problem. Competitors have no chance against Microsoft, so Microsoft collects rents, but the rents are kept minimal because Microsoft knows that as soon as they let a competitor into their market, the situation could change quickly. So for Microsoft it is not so much the reality of competition but the threat of competition that keeps the rents reasonable, unlike our Carnegie Hall carpenter who has no threats due to the union.

Another example of a legitimate or open-market monopoly is Amazon. Amazon is a public company but Jeff Bezos, the founder of Amazon, runs the company like a private domain. For example, Amazon exists on the fringes of profitability, making just enough profit to stay in business. The reason is that Jeff Bezos wants to do to retailing what Sam Walton, the founder of Walmart, did to retailing: make not incremental but revolutionary change.

Sam Walton changed retailing by simply declaring that instead of working for the manufacturers to distribute their products on their terms, he, Sam Walton, had the customers, not them, and that he would make the rules. If the manufacturers wanted Sam to retail their products, they would play by his rules. This must have seemed ridiculous to the manufacturers in the beginning, but Sam won and today the manufacturers travel from cities like Cincinnati, Chicago and New York to Bentonville, Arkansas, to learn how to present their wares to fit the Walmart inventory system.

Jeff Bezos has another idea: he has the customers like Sam, but he wants to save them a trip to a Walmart store. As the Yellow Pages ad used to say, *"Just let your fingers do the walking."* Jeff's idea is that people will just visit the Amazon website and with a few mouse-clicks complete the purchase. The next step is for Amazon to deliver the purchase, which Jeff Bezos has expedited by making a deal with the U.S. Postal Service to even deliver Amazon packages on Sundays; in his latest initiative, Jeff is exploring delivery by drone. Obviously, Jeff is a revolutionary thinker and his investors are perfectly happy with his decisions and management objectives. The role that Amazon commands in retailing is reaching monopoly proportions but at the cost of very thin profits. But some day, Jeff Bezos may drive off all competitors and then begin collecting rents, at least for a while. In the meantime, society benefits from Amazon's drive for monopoly.

What the Carnegie Hall carpenter, Walmart, Microsoft and Amazon all have in common is pricing power from market power – beating weaker competitors, or in the case of the Carnegie Hall carpenter, no competitors. But rent collection is an analog value, from zero to a very large number, and in fractional increments. What can be said with certainty is that they are all rent seekers, as is everybody, but only the carpenter has done it by skirting competition. And so the difference is that the carpenter's rent has added no value to society, whereas the corporate rents Microsoft, Walmart and Amazon are seeking and collecting have come in the wake of a great deal of value produced for the common good.

Corporate Governance in Germany

In Germany there are two legal forms of incorporation for large stock companies: AG and GmbH. AG stands for *Aktiengesellschaft*.

GmbH stands for *Gesellschaft mit beschränkter Haftung* which means company with limited liability. And company means people or members – a company of people are members (*gesellschaft*). *Aktien* means shares and refers to the members or people holding shares. I just stick to AG and GmbH and mostly focus on AG which is the German equivalent of a U.S. "C" corporation.

The following material comes directly from the SGL Group website:

> *German corporate governance fundamentals and practices are generally based on the provisions of the German Stock Corporation Act (Aktiengesetz), the German Codetermination Act (Mitbestimmungsgesetz), and the German Corporate Governance Code.*
>
> *German stock corporations have three corporate bodies in Germany: an annual general meeting of shareholders, a board of management (Vorstand) and a senior supervisory board (Aufsichtsrat).* (The Vorstand is just the senior management and the German counterpart to CEO and senior officers of a corporation.)
>
> *At the annual general meeting, shareholders exercise the rights granted to them by the Stock Corporation Act. These include, in particular, the resolution on the appropriation of net retained profits* (to dividends, etc.), *the election of the auditor, the discharge of the board of management and the senior supervisory board, amendments to the Articles of Incorporation, the issue of new stock and convertible bonds and bonds with warrants, the authorization to acquire own stock* (their own "Treasury Stock,"stock in what in the U.S. is called a "stock buyback"), *structural changes like transformations or enterprise contracts, and the election of the shareholders' representatives to the senior supervisory board.*
>
> *The German Stock Corporation Act ... calls for a clear separation of duties between management and supervisory functions and therefore prohibits simultaneous membership on*

both boards (not to mention combining the office of CEO with any of the boards and certainly never as Chairman of a supervisory body). *Members of the board of management and the senior supervisory board must exercise the standard of care of a prudent and diligent business person when carrying out their duties. In complying with this standard of care, members must not only take into account the interests of shareholders, as would typically be the case with a U.S. board of directors, but also the interests of other constituents, such as the company's employees, and, to some extent, the broader public interest.*

It should be noted here that in Germany the corporation has a duty to benefit the country and the country's population as a whole, and employees as well as the stockholders. In the U.S. the corporation has no other function than to benefit stockholders. The corporation has a legal obligation to make a profit from which the stockholders benefit.

In Germany, the board of management (Vostand) is responsible for managing the company and representing it in its dealings with third parties:

The board of management's functions are comparable to those performed in the ordinary course of business by the senior executives of a U.S. company. However, the members of the board of management of a German stock corporation, are regarded as peers and share a collective responsibility for all management decisions. (In the U.S. the CEO is the undisputed leader, and in many cases the next in line of management has very little influence in corporate decision making.)

The supervisory board (Aufsichtsrat) oversees the company's board of management and appoints its members. Members of the supervisory board may generally not be involved in the day-to-day management of the company. However, the company's articles of incorporation must specify those matters of fundamental importance which may only be dealt with upon the prior consent of the supervisory board; the supervisory board may specify further matters which require its consent. Matters requiring such prior consent usually include decisions or actions having a fundamental impact on the assets, financial or profit situation of the company.

The supervisory boards (Aufsichtsrat) of major German stock corporations are subject to employee codetermination and are comprised of representatives of the shareholders and employees. Traditionally, the shareholder representatives on the supervisory board have a good understanding of the business activities of the company. Depending on the company's total number of employees, up to one-half of the supervisory board members will be elected by the company's employees. The chairman of the Supervisory Board is a representative of the shareholders, and the deputy chairman or one of the two deputy chairmen is a representative of the employees. In the event of a tie vote, the deciding vote is cast by the chairman.

In recent times, there has been a trend towards selecting shareholder representatives for supervisory boards from a wider spectrum of candidates, including representatives from non-German companies, in an effort to introduce a broader range of experience and expertise and a larger degree in independence. Under the keyword "diversity", discussions on proper corporate governance have recently also focused on an appropriate representation of females on the supervisory board.

German law also has several rules applicable to supervisory board members which are designed to ensure a certain degree of independence of the board members. In addition to prohibiting members of the board of management from serving on the supervisory board, German law requires members of the supervisory board to act in the best interest of the company. They do not have to follow direction or instruction from third parties. Any service, consulting or similar agreements between the company and any of its supervisory board members must be approved by the supervisory board.

The German Stock Corporation Act and the further regulations do not require the creation of specific supervisory board committees. The Corporate Governance Code recommends, however, that the supervisory board establish an audit committee to handle the appointment of the company's independent auditor once he has been approved by the annual general meeting of shareholders. The audit committee also addresses issues of accounting, risk management, compliance and auditor independence.

Furthermore, the Code recommends the creation of a nomination committee to be composed exclusively of shareholders' representatives, which proposes suitable candidates to the supervisory board for its recommendations for election to the General Meeting.

In the majority of the German stock companies, supervisory boards have also formed other committees to make the work of the supervisory board more efficient. For instance, a personnel committee is often installed to deal with the compensation of board members and nomination issues. Members of the supervisory board elected by the employees may serve on any committee established by the supervisory board (with the exception of the nomination committee), but an equal participation of shareholder- and employee representatives is not prescribed. All committee members as well as the chairman of the supervisory board are elected by the supervisory board itself and not by the annual general meeting of shareholders.

The above model of German corporate governance is a dramatic departure from U.S. practice and defines a much more collaborative environment, in that no single person has overarching authority over the assets and operation of the corporation. There are two differences that are a particularly dramatic departure from U.S. practice. First, the inability to combine the office of Chairman (shareholders‘ representative) and CEO. The other difference is the more broad-based selection of auditor in the German corporation – the choice is approved by the shareholders.

The role of the Auditor

One area that gets attention in the U.S. from time to time but always seems to fade away as an issue is the role of "independent" auditor. The company maintains its own records in an accounting department that might be quite vast in a larger S&P 500 corporation. In the U.S., publicly listed corporations are required to file quarterly reports which reduce down to three quarterly reports called 10-Ks, which are usually printed on ordinary copier paper, and one annual report that typically resembles a glossy fashion magazine.

The gloss of course is to bewilder the already bewildered investor. The report will begin with a message from the CEO. This will be in the style of a letter written home by a soldier on the front reporting on how much progress has been made in totally vanquishing the enemy who will soon come to his senses and lie prostrate on the field begging for mercy.

Next will be a description of the business with lots of glossy pictures of company products and company plant and equipment. Then it is on to the financial reporting which will contain, among other tabulations, three tabulations required by law: Income Statement, Balance Sheet and Statement of Changes in Financial Position. Be very careful about the data that you see. What counts is the data that you don't see (see Enron, above). The data are carefully articulated in such a way as to put the rosiest picture on actual results.

Then, in case there are any wary investors left who have an uncomfortable but unidentified feeling of unease, there is the "independent" auditor's opinion to help guide that uneasy investor. The auditor's statement pretty much follows a standard script as follows: *"We have examined the financial statements of XYZ company and feel the statements fairly represent the state of the company."* Now here comes the best part. The "independent" outside auditing firm is almost always one of a group of six or more globally recognized prestigious accounting firms that are acknowledged to be so prestigious that their pronouncements cannot be questioned. And to top it all off, they are hired by the people they are auditing! Do you smell a rat here? The SEC doesn't. They think it smells like roses. Of course, the SEC has been captured!

Arthur Andersen & Enron

Below is a 2002 report from ABC News relating the events surrounding the last days of Arthur Andersen, whom Ken Lay had hired to audit their reports at Enron:

> The U.S. Justice Department today announced the indictment of embattled accounting firm Arthur Andersen on one count of obstruction of justice relating to the collapse of former energy giant Enron Corp. A federal grand jury actually filed the indictment on March 7, but it was unsealed today.

> "The firm sought to undermine our justice system by destroying evidence," said Deputy Attorney General Larry Thompson at an afternoon news conference, saying the firm has intentionally disposed of "tons" of evidence after a government inquiry began last October. He added: "At the time, Andersen knew full well that these documents were relevant."

> Andersen, however, has made it clear it will not plead guilty to the charge, having already rejected a plea bargain deal with the government. The company released a vigorous response to the announcement this afternoon, calling the Justice Department's actions "without precedent and an extraordinary abuse of prosecutorial discretion," and "a gross abuse of government power."

> Charges Based on Shredding. The obstruction charge is based on claims that Andersen employees shredded important documents about Enron's finances, even though

they knew the Securities and Exchange Commission was formally looking into Enron. The Justice Department also alleges Andersen employees deleted relevant computer files.

Andersen's basic line of defense is that the shredding was conducted in the company's Houston office under the supervision of David Duncan, the firm's lead partner in charge of Enron's audits, and was not ordered by executives at Andersen headquarters in Chicago. An Andersen internal report, written by two law firms and obtained today by ABCNEWS, emphasizes this point.

At the time of the shredding in October, says the report, "Duncan and the other partners on the Enron engagement knew that the SEC had made an informal request to Enron for documents and information relating to partnerships involving Enron's former CFO, Andrew Fastow, and that private civil lawsuits had also been filed."

But the indictment charges the document destruction was widespread and involved employees at multiple locations, including Andersen's London office.
"The obstruction effort was not just confined to a few isolated individuals or documents," said Thompson. "This was a substantial undertaking over an extended period of time with a very wide scope." Duncan's lawyers released a statement this afternoon saying that he "continues to cooperate with all of the ongoing investigations" and would not comment on Andersen's indictment.

On Jan. 10, Andersen acknowledged it had destroyed thousands of Enron-related documents and e-mails last fall, as investigations into the events that ultimately led to the company's bankruptcy were under way. Enron, after filing the largest-ever U.S. bankruptcy on Dec. 2, fired Andersen on Jan. 17.

The maximum potential punishment for the charge is a five-year probation term for Arthur Andersen and a $500,000 fine.

Multiple Reasons for Indictment

In another letter released Wednesday night by Andersen, the firm defends itself and strongly criticizes the Justice Department's line of inquiry into the Enron matter.

So there you have it, a major U.S. iconic corporation hijacked by a CEO and Chairman, blowing through full disclosure in financial reporting and getting help from a very prestigious accounting firm hired to audit the books. Where was the board in all of this? As with many boards of U.S. corporations, totally irrelevant. The iconic accounting firm Arthur Andersen, incidentally, no longer exists. For one thing, how good would a pronouncement of good financial health from Arthur Andersen be? Probably not good enough to overcome general investor paranoia.

Finding Your Way

What you have been exposed to is a comparison of two very different approaches to corporate governance which are rooted in two very different cultures, Germany and the United States. German history is marked by cooperation in early guilds to protect the skills of different trades and then the formation of a commercial partnership among a group of cities like the Hanseatic League. German culture is one of cooperation to achieve a common good.

By contrast, U.S. culture venerates the individual with a history that focuses on the great accomplishments of great individuals. The CEO in a German corporation is a team member, while the CEO is a U.S. corporation is a gunslinger out to singlehandedly defeat the competition. The job of the board is to pick the right gunslinger and then make sure he or she doesn't hijack the store. Sometimes the board fails and you have an Enron. Sometimes it is not only the board but the employees helping themselves and you have a General Motors failure. In both cases, unlike Germany where it is all "We, We, We," in American corporations it is all "Me, Me, Me." Germany is a nation-state of collaboration. The United States is a free-for-all.

American culture was not always so prone to go off the rails; there was a time in recent history when there was something called an American "establishment" and the country was more or less ruled by a WASP (White Anglo-Saxon Protestant) culture that spread out from the born WASPs to the "wannabe" WASPs.

The ethos of WASP culture was to strive for order rather than wealth. If the universe was well-ordered the outcome would be the "best of all possible worlds." And to bring about that end, one must live and exhibit a life of restraint and be a steward of all of society. It all worked because the WASPs were in charge, and those who wanted to be in charge would perceive their path to success in being WASP-like. So a well-ordered world was brought about, perhaps reaching its zenith with the period following World War II. Those who were not WASPs were respectful of those who were and everybody had a job to do.

With the ramping up of the economy after WWII, wealth became more widely distributed and soon the WASPs and WASP wannabes were overrun by a brash new society who wanted to *"...beat the blue-bloods at their own game."* And they succeeded, going to the best schools and living in the best houses in the best neighborhoods and sending their children to the best schools; but they missed the core of WASP culture, the part about being stewards of society. Their financial success soon became their identity and society be damned; what was society but their society anyway?

These new upstarts didn't understand that it was society that built the roads and built the schools and built the infrastructure that allowed 300 million Americans to go out and buy their wares – they thought it was all them and that if anything, they were responsible for the infrastructure; if they paid themselves enough, they wouldn't need 300 million Americans, they would buy it all themselves.

So what at one time what was a revered American culture that saved the world from a totalitarian future and dropped Hershey chocolate bars with parachutes from planes over the defeated foe's principal city of Berlin, has morphed into remote indiscriminate killing by drone machine, where exploding missiles in wedding processions are dismissed as an unpleasant, but necessary "collateral damage" to "Keep America Safe." Yes, in America, the WASPs with their sense of community and personal restraint no longer rule.

The point must be made that in the U.S. there is unprecedented diversity; each corporation has its own unique culture, and there are many U.S. corporations that are hugely successful even in cases where the office of Chairman and CEO are combined. What keeps it all together is a U.S. infrastructure that provides educated consumers with jobs and incomes and some corporate cultures where everybody at the corporation is vigilant about malfeasance in office. U.S.-style corporate governance allows for the uniquely talented to work their magic on a corporation, resulting in outsize performance but at the risk of, in the case of Enron, losing it all. The best approach is to scrutinize corporate governance carefully but also to put some German companies in a well-diversified portfolio.

Also, there are cases of out-of-control board members forcing action that hurts the corporation they are stewards of. One case is JC Penney, where a prominent board member forced the hiring of a high-profile CEO he knew or knew of. The new CEO fired the old management team and brought in his own people. After a series of bad decisions and dwindling sales, the new CEO was eventually fired, along with his team. The old CEO was brought back and the prominent board member resigned. It is an open question whether JC Penney will fully recover, but the brand is strong enough to have inspired the issuance of 84 million new shares of stock, which will keep it afloat until they can find the inspired new leadership the company needs.

JCP is a classic case of the role of corporate governance in the health of the company and the role brand plays in keeping the company afloat during periods when the right management goes missing.

GMI Metrics

A number of third-party organizations have weighed in on these governance issues:

- The Corporate Library
- Institutional Shareholder Services (ISS)
- Governance Metrics International (GMI)

These organizations publish ratings on companies. As in the Enron case with Arthur Andersen auditing, there have been misses. An example is a company rated in the upper 35% of all rated companies and in the upper 8% of peer companies. The company was later discovered to have falsified financial statements, overstating earnings by $1.4 billion. The company's subterfuge and crime reinforce the point that structure does not trump culture. Presence of an independent board alone does not guarantee success. It is a culture devoted to fair dealing, or as in the case of German companies and Japanese companies like Toyota, a culture of "Us" and not "Me." So in U.S. culture, the need for outside rating remains.

On the following pages are exhibits relating to corporate governance. First is a 2007 table of ratings, alphabetically by country, for 36 international corporations published by Governance Metrics International (GMI).The GMI ratings are 0 to 10 with 10 being the highest. Their website states:

Our flagship service, GMI Analyst, is a comprehensive web-based platform providing research, ratings, real-time updates, robust search functionality and analytical tools to help clients assess issuer risk. The research platform provides:

- *ESG ratings, research and real-time updates on about 5,500 companies worldwide based on 120 carefully selected risk factors (ESG KeyMetrics™)*
- *AGR® ratings, research and real-time updates on about 18,000 companies worldwide based on more than 50 discrete risk factors*

- *Environmental performance data from Trucost, the world's leading provider of comparative data on corporate environmental impacts, including Greenhouse Gases (GHGs), water, waste, pollutants and natural resource dependency.*
- *Unique data on litigation and financial-distress risk*
- *Daily and weekly updates, quarterly ratings reviews and event-driven analysis*
- *Robust search functionality, screening and analytical tools, including WatchLists, Portfolio Analysis, Alerts, Industry Browser, peer-group analysis and historical data on AGR risk*

Governance Metrics International: Ratings on International Corporations (2007)

Company	GMI Rating	Country
BHP Billiton	9.5	Australia
InBev	4.5	Belgium
Banco Bradesco	3.5	Brazil
Royal Bank of Canada	10.0	Canada
PetroChina	1.5	China
Dansk Bank Group	7.0	Denmark
Nokia	9.0	Finland
Michelin	3.0	France
BMW Group	7.0	Germany
Infosys	7.5	India
ENI	8.0	Italy
Sony	7.0	Japan
Toyota Motor Corp.	4.5	Japan
Kuala Lumpur Kepong	5.0	Malaysia
Aegon	7.0	Netherlands
Heineken Holdings	1.5	Netherlands
Norsk Hydro	6.5	Norway
Gazprom	4.5	Russia
Flextronics International	7.5	Singapore
Posco	5.5	South Korea

Samsung Electronics	4.0	South Korea
Banco Santander	7.5	Spain
Ericsson	6.5	Sweden
UBS	6.0	Switzerland
Hon Hai Precision Ind.	4.5	Taiwan
Bangkok Bank	6.0	Thailand
Turkcell Iletisim Hizmetleri	6.0	Turkey
BP	8.5	United Kingdom
HSBC	8.0	United Kingdom
Royal Dutch Shell	8.0	UK/Netherlands
Unilever	10.0	UK/Netherlands
General Electric	8.5	United States
Johnson & Johnson	9.0	United States
Microsoft	8.0	United States
Procter & Gamble	10.0	United States
Washington Post	7.0	United States

GMI also flags companies where the CEO makes more than three times the median pay for the other named executive officers (NEOs). In the words of GMI:

If a large pay differential is justified by the relative value of the executives' contributions, it suggests that the company in question has a "weak bench" and may struggle with internal succession planning if the CEO needs to be replaced. On the other hand, if the other named executive officers are in fact near-equal partners with the CEO, the latter is being overpaid for his or her work. This overpayment is both a misuse of shareholder resources and a potential source of poor morale in the executive team.

As of August 2012 the companies listed among those companies cited for Internal Pay Equity issues were:

Company Name	Ticker
Lorillard Inc.	LO
Deere & Company	DE
Avery Dennison Corp.	AVY
CBS Corporation	CBS
The Hain Celestial Group	HAIN
Tupperware Brands Corp.	TUP
Johnson Controls, Inc.	JCI
Big Lots, Inc.	BIG
Pitney Bowes Inc.	PBI
Rock-Tenn Company	RKT

Following is a recent (2013) table of a GMI Accounting and Governance Risk (AGR®) survey of 100 companies provided by the financial magazine Forbes. I have added columns for beta and dividend yield.

The value of this table is that it lists smaller companies and Publicly Traded Partnerships, including REITs and pipelines, to help with constructing a more broadly-diversified portfolio. I hesitate to invest in smaller companies because they usually operate in markets that are faster moving and not part of everyday life, like Coca-Cola for example, and need more vigorous tracking; then the question arises, is the decline due to structural faults or is it just the market jitters? So I like to leave small company investing to the experts who manage mutual funds or index funds which are offered to the public as an alternative to individual stocks. This is discussed more fully later on.

But as an alternative to funds, high GMI ratings give me a level of confidence to invest in discrete companies, which is preferred if you can do it – GMI ratings allow us to dip our toe into the small-cap world. See GMI ratings beginning on the following page. A perfect score is 100 so look for the highest GMI ratings score.

	COMPANY	TICKER	INDUSTRY	Avg. AGR Score	BETA	DIV YIELD %
			LARGE CAP			
1	Cincinnati Financial	CINF	Insurance	97	0.80	5.20
2	Enbridge Energy Partners, LP	EEP	MLP	84	0.76	8.80
3	Essex Property Trust	ESS	REIT	94	1.07	3.10
4	Kimco Realty	KIM	REIT	91	1.51	5.50
5	NetSuite	N	Software	99	1.70	
6	PartnerRe	PRE	Insurance	89	1.07	2.90
7	Realty Income	O	REIT	87	0.62	5.70
8	Unum Group	UNM	Insurance		1.46	1.90
9	Valero Energy	VLO	Energy	89	2.72	2.50
			MID-CAP			
10	Alnylam Pharmaceuticals	ALNY	Pharma	88	2.66	
11	American Campus Communities	ACC	REIT	89	0.21	4.40
12	American Eagle Outfitters	AEO	Retail	95	0.59	3.10
13	Aspen Insurance Holdings	AHL	Insurance	96	0.78	2.30
14	Associated BancCorp	ASBC	Bank	89	1.82	2.20
15	Athenahealth	ATHN	IT	91	0.66	
16	Atlas Pipeline Partners LP	APL	MLP	88	0.94	7.00
17	Boise Cascade	BCC	Paper	99		
18	Brandywine Realty Trust	BDN	REIT	92	1.62	4.30
19	BRE Properties	BRE	REIT	92	1.06	3.00
20	Casey's General Stores	CASY	Retail	92	0.60	1.00
21	Columbia Sportswear	COLM	Apparel	98	1.23	1.50
22	Energy XXI	EXXI	Energy	91	2.33	1.70
23	First American Financial	FAF	Insurance	92	0.85	1.90

24	Fortress Investment Group	FIG	Financial	90	2.47	2.90
25	Glacier Bancorp	GBCI	Bank	88	1.75	2.10
26	Government Properties Income Trust	GOV	REIT	96	0.94	6.90
27	Highwoods Properties	HIW	REIT	91	1.17	4.70
28	Infinity Pharmaceuticals	INFI	Pharma	88	0.72	
29	Insulet	PODD	Medical	95	1.11	
30	Jones Lang LaSalle	JLL	Financial	93	2.16	0.40
31	Herman Miller	MLHR	Wholesale	91	1.75	1.70
32	Northwest Natural Gas	NWN	Utility	92	0.27	4.30
33	NorthWestern Corp.	NWE	Utility	89	0.50	3.40
34	Old Dominion Freight Line	ODFL	Transportation	89	1.31	
35	Old Republic International	ORI	Insurance	93	0.83	4.10
36	Patterson Companies	PDCO	Medical	88	0.88	1.50
37	Portland General Electric	POR	Utility	94	0.43	3.70
38	Post Properties	PPS	REIT	99	0.70	3.00
39	PriceSmart	PSMT	Retail	95	0.85	0.50
40	Reinsurance Group of America	RGA	Insurance	96	1.43	1.60
41	Sauer-Danfoss	private	Industrial	94		
42	Selective Insurance Group	SIGI	Insurance	93	1.43	1.90
43	Vector Group	VGR	Tobacco	88	0.21	9.80
	SMALL CAP					
44	Acadia Pharmaceuticals	ACAD	Pharma	88	3.77	
45	Altra Holdings	AIMC	Industrial	88	2.06	1.30
46	American Railcar Industries	ARII	Industrial	92	2.97	2.30

47	Amerisafe	AMSF	Insurance	91	0.92	0.80
48	Apogee Enterprises	APOG	Industrial	93	1.75	1.00
49	Arrow Financial	AROW	Bank	88	0.32	3.70
50	Camden National	CAC	Bank	98	0.83	3.10
51	Capstone Turbine	CPST	Industrial	99	1.83	
52	Carmike Cinemas	CKEC	Retail	92	0.20	9.10
53	Columbus McKinnon	CMCO	Industrial	90	2.32	
54	Cooper-Standard Holdings	CPS	Industrial	88	0.87	
55	Daktronics	DAKT	Wholesale	99	1.30	1.60
56	Destination Maternity	DEST	Retail	89	1.74	2.40
57	Donegal Group	DGICA	Insurance	98	-0.01	3.10
58	EMC Insurance Group	EMCI	Insurance	96	0.49	3.40
59	First Busey	BUSE	Bank	96	1.00	3.70
60	First Commonwealth Financial	FCF	Bank	94	1.65	2.80
61	First Interstate Bancsystem	FIBK	Bank	94	1.37	1.75
62	First National Bank Alaska	FBAK	Bank	92	0.23	2.80
63	Flushing Financial	FFIC	Bank	96	1.04	4.00
64	Gorman-Rupp	GRC	Industrial	97	1.02	1.40
65	Hanmi Financial	HAFC	Bank	91	1.97	1.00
66	Haverty Furniture Companies	HVT	Retail	88	1.07	2.20
67	Hawkins	HWKN	Chemical	89	1.02	2.10
68	Horace Mann Educators	HMN	Insurance	96	1.60	2.80
69	Incontact Inc.	SAAS	Software	91	1.30	
70	Kimball International	KBALB	Semiconductor	98	1.73	2.90
71	La-Z-Boy	LZB	Wholesale	89	1.90	2.20
72	LMI Aerospace	LMIA	Aerospace	91	1.73	
73	MAP	acquired	Pharma	94		

	Pharmaceuticals					
74	Marcus	MCS	Retail	91	0.59	2.80
75	Meridien Bioscience	VIVO	Biotechnology	89	1.38	3.60
76	Methode Electronics	MEI	Industrial	91	1.65	2.90
77	Myers Industries	MYE	Chemical	90	0.89	2.50
78	National Interstate	NATL	Insurance	99	0.60	1.50
79	Navigators Group	NAVG	Insurance	95	0.42	
80	Northfield Bancorp	NFBK	Bank	91	0.03	2.00
81	Patriot Transportation Holding	PATR	Transportation	93	1.25	
82	SY Bancorp	SYBT	Bank	91	1.00	3.10
83	Safety Insurance Group	SAFT	Insurance	96	0.89	4.60
84	Sandy Spring Bancorp	SASR	Bank	93	1.14	2.00
85	Shenandoah Communications	SHEN	Telecom	95	2.17	1.90
86	Spartan Stores	SPTN	Retail	94	0.70	1.40
87	Spectranetics	SPNC	Medical	94	0.99	
88	State Auto Financial	STFC	Insurance	92	0.94	3.20
89	Triple-S Management	GTS	Insurance	88	1.35	
90	Tropicana Entertainment	TPCA	Casino	92		
91	United Financial Bancorp	UBNK	Bank	93	0.79	2.20
92	United Fire Group	UFCS	Insurance	99	0.03	2.70
93	Universal Truckload Services	UACL	Transportation	96	1.44	0.75
94	Vical	VICL	Pharma	91	2.62	
95	Virginia Commerce Bancorp	VCBI	Bank	97	0.89	

96	West Marine	WMAR	Retail	93	1.32	
97	World Wrestling Entertainment	WWE	Retail	94	0.76	4.00
	MICRO CAP					
98	Cambridge Bancorp	CATC	Bank	98	0.37	3.50
99	Furmanite	FRM	Wholesale	88	1.84	
100	Nature's Sunshine Products	NATR	Pharma	92	0.61	2.20

These GMI ratings give me a sense of greater comfort in making investments in large capitalization companies, but they are particularly useful in making investments in small companies. Small companies are less visible and more difficult to study as investment candidates.

Since a widely-diversified portfolio might contain some small company content, the solution is to just invest in a small-company mutual fund or index fund and let the fund managers do the work for you. The problem with funds is that they impose three sources of drag on performance: (1) underperforming components to add bulk (2) fees and (3) churning. Index funds have reduced fees and churning down to a level where they are actually a good value for the oversight they offer.

Churning is the frequent turnover of fund constituents by frequent trading that often is more shortsighted than profitable. Index funds address this drawback as well with much more stable fund management. Nevertheless, all funds feel a requirement to hold so many positions that there is very little discrimination between stellar-performing companies and companies that are just getting along. The overall result is muted and investors are better off with a much smaller group of companies within the sector. GMI ratings provide the kind of insight into small companies that might allow for individual small company selection over a third-party fund.

Chapter 6

The Stock Market

IN ORDER TO RAISE MONEY to start a company, entrepreneurs turn to the "capital markets" for sources of investment. In some cases, if the cash requirements are not too great, a "private-placement" will be sought; for example, a very large financial firm like an insurance company buys all the stock of a new company for what they feel is an attractive price, calculated on the market size and the company's relative strength in serving that market. After the company succeeds, the stock may be sold to the public in what is called an *Initial Public Offering* (IPO).

Most new ventures begin with an entrepreneur getting "seed" money from families and friends. When this source dries up, then larger sources like insurance companies may be invited to buy out the early investors and take over ownership of the new enterprise. Eventually, cash needs may outstrip even the large financier and the company must go to the public for financing via IPO.

Once the public has purchased all the shares of the new venture, then all further share purchases and dispositions take place on the secondary market we know as the stock market. This is how commerce is financed.

Investors' appetite for share ownership may vary with changing conditions. If banks and other credit (bond) issuers are paying high interest rates in order to borrow money, some investors will move money from the stock market to the bond market and the stock market will slump in capitalization as sellers overwhelm buyers. During periods of social unrest, as in war, money will move away from the market to safer places, like gold, a store of value in troubled times. So total market capitalization fluctuates, with conditions generally alternating between very high valuation, which may be thought of as "overbought," to very low valuations that may be thought of as "oversold." In any case, stock prices fluctuate and it is up to each investor to decide what a reasonable price is for every stock they are considering.

Liquidity

In addition to profitability, there will be one other crucial issue for investors - how quickly can they convert their stock purchases back to cash? As you might imagine, even stock issues felt to have great promise are not invested in if money is locked up for long periods with no way out. All investors feel this way, so in addition to profitability, "liquidity" is a must to attract investment. Investors must be reassured that they may freely convert stock to cash at any time. Consequently, stock may not be listed on an exchange unless it can be demonstrated that there is sufficient demand for the stock – trading thresholds must be met. If a stock that has been trading successfully experiences a significant drop in demand, then it may be de-listed by the exchange to protect new buyers from buying an issue they cannot readily sell.

In addition to the overall market movement between highs and lows brought on by more generalized economic conditions, like fluctuating interest rates, individual company issues also are subject to buying and selling pressures brought on by changing prospects of future profitability. Many new businesses are started to exploit some new technological development, and if successful in the early stages may reach the point of issuing an initial public offering. But at this point there may be more promise than reality to the prospects, and from there the enterprise may grow and go mainstream or may wither and die.

The Case for Acquisitions

If the company survives, the next stage is buyout by a major corporation interested in filling a gap in their product line. The small company is hemmed in by larger, better-financed rivals so being acquired by a large player provides immediate access to larger markets and makes the company more valuable. When the buyout is first announced, the stock of the newer company will usually jump to a much higher valuation justified by the greater profit that broader market access will bring.

An example might be a new chocolate bar that succeeds in gaining a share of the market. Retailers won't give the new chocolate bar company much shelf space because they know that Hershey and Nestle and other chocolate suppliers are proven revenue generators, so they get the best shelf space. But Hershey may decide to buy the new chocolate bar company because they feel it makes a good addition to their product line.

Once the new chocolate bar is marketed by Hershey, retailers will give the new chocolate bar more and better shelf space. Here is a case where the same business is worth more as a Hershey brand than as an independent brand. The stock market will drive up the stock price of the new company, and sometimes ahead of the buyout announcement just on the expectation that such a buyout is probable.

Not all buyouts are successful, however. In a similar and well-publicized case, Nabisco bought out the Stella D'Oro cookie company in what may have seemed a marriage made in heaven. The original family that started the business in 1930 sold the business in 1992 to Nabisco for $100 million. Nabisco then went through its own buyout to Kraft Foods which sold the Stella D'Oro business in 2006 for $17.5 million to a private equity firm. Obviously something happened; Nabisco seems not to have succeeded in leveraging its market power to benefit its Stella D'Oro business. So what may seem like a no-brainer doesn't always play out as you might expect.

Buying Common Stock

The New York Stock Exchange, the Big Board, lists over 8,000 common stocks of public corporations. The National Association of Securities Dealers Automated Quotations (NASDAQ) lists around 3,300 common stocks. Between the two exchanges an investor has a choice of over 11,000 issues with daily trading volume in the billions of shares – opportunity and liquidity galore.

Given this amount of choice and liquidity, it is natural that those individuals willing to spend more time following the markets will gain a sense of empowerment in forecasting stock price appreciation, and for them the stock market is like a non-stop amusement park. But shares cannot be directly bought and sold; intermediaries with access to buyers and sellers must be used. So organizations have sprung up to cater to this market, mainly stock brokerage businesses. An investor must open an account at a brokerage and then direct the brokerage to buy and sell shares for his or her account.

Most investors don't have the time to follow market action on a daily basis, so the brokerage houses employ stock analysts that report regularly on the prospects of the stock issues they cover. Usually an analyst will cover a particular sector like airlines, pharmaceuticals, banks, automobiles, retailers and so on. An investor may then, as a customer of a brokerage house, access these analyst reports that usually are categorized by attractiveness and volatility. For example, analyst reports may rate a company's stock a "buy" with "low volatility" or "high volatility." *Volatility* refers to the price behavior of the stock: smooth ride to the top or bumpy ride with breathtaking tumbles. Usually there are three attractiveness ratings: "buy," "neutral" and "sell." Volatility ratings will usually be either "high" or "low."

Many investors don't even have time for this level of stock study and so simply use a stock broker employed by the firm to manage their account. The account may then be managed in one of two ways: with or without "discretion." *Discretion* is the status given to a broker to trade in a client's account on the client's behalf without consulting the client. Many brokers stay away from this level of responsibility and offer only "non-discretionary" accounts. It would not be unusual for an aggrieved client to sue a broker who was given discretion and then lost a large portion of the assets. Actually, the brokerage would be sued since they have "deeper pockets," something the brokerage houses are keenly aware of and take steps to head off.

Brokers who offer discretionary accounts are heavily screened by the brokerage house and heavily monitored. In such cases, a client selects an investment "style" and then the brokerage house tracks every trade to make sure it conforms to the style selected by the client. If the client loses money but the style was adhered to, the client doesn't have a case and it can all be proven by recordkeeping on the part of the brokerage house.

Several styles a client may select are: "Conservative," "Aggressive," "Contrarian" and "Income." There are more and they vary from brokerage to brokerage. In addition to specific rules governing discretionary accounts, there are more generalized rules governing all accounts.

Know Your Customer

The cardinal rule is "Know Your Customer." At one time known as Rule 405, it requires that all account opening documents require the client to disclose information that will enable the broker to discriminate between suitable and unsuitable investment recommendations. Mostly the suitability factor is making sure that the client will have enough liquid cash to meet emergencies and to head off any preemptive selling at a loss to meet obligations. A person with few assets, for example, would not be offered a volatile stock for fear that near-term depressed price would come at a time when the assets were needed for something urgent. In this case, a stock with less promise but also less expected volatility would be a better choice. If the stock needed to be sold in an emergency the likelihood is that there would either be no loss, or a small loss.

Wealthy clients, under the "Know Your Customer" rule, may, if they elect "Aggressive" style, be offered speculative issues that have great promise, but may be expected to weather an extended period of depressed valuation while they wait for the underlying business to succeed and have that success reflected in appreciating stock price.

Whether the client is rich or poor the same "Know Your Customer" rule applies, but the relationship is always one of a "broker" or a facilitator of stock ownership for profit. The incentive for the broker is to see the client do well so that the client buys even more stock on which the broker may charge a fee, often commissions, for buying and selling shares of stock.

If a client is not entirely comfortable with this level of care, there is a higher level which is called "Fiduciary." A fiduciary has an obligation to place the client's interest ahead of his or her own. These are gray areas but it would be difficult to conceive fiduciary taking on a client who wanted an Aggressive style in investment. A fiduciary relationship implies that money will not be lost unless the client insists upon buying a speculative issue over the objections of his financial advisor.

In fact, money is lost all the time because the markets are random and forward-looking, and just as it is not possible to pick the winners with any regularity so it is not possible to exclude the losers with any regularity. Also, investors will invest in what they know and they know more about the stocks they research, so research necessarily leads to purchases. In fact, it may be stated that stocks are researched not to exclude them, but to buy them – stocks are researched until a buy decision on them can be reached. This is because you can make a good case out of any business thesis.

In the world of intermediaries there are brokerage houses and asset management firms. Brokerages are staffed by "Registered Representatives" known as stock brokers or Financial Advisors and have no more obligation to their clients than to offer only suitable investments by the "Know Your Customer" rule, which today is known as FINRA rule 2090.

FINRA, the Financial Industry Regulatory Authority, issues rules governing operation of public financial markets, an authority given them by the SEC, the

Securities & Exchange Commission. This all got started by the Franklin Delano Roosevelt administration in 1939 following the great stock market crash of 1929. It was felt that the crash was caused by unscrupulous stock market practices that needed to be cleaned up. The ultimate cleaner-upper was a gentleman named Ferdinand Pecora, whose actions prompted creation of the SEC and the passage of a number of laws regulating financial services, including the suitability rule "Know Your Customer."

The World of Investors

The opportunity to make money in the stock market draws many people into the market in hopes of realizing quick gains. But the market is totally random; the expected outcome from this would be a number of losses offsetting a number of gains to arrive, after a period, at zero gain/loss. But while the market is random, people are not; they react to gains by increasing their trading activity and react to losses by reducing their trading activity. This lopsided reaction leads to losses, since gains are reinvested up until the time they become losses, at which point trading stops. So while the market will continue to gain and lose, investors mostly will wind up with losses.

The only way to come out with a gain is to engage in a mechanical process that admits to the randomness of the market and admits that randomness cannot be calculated. However, for many, the allure of gaining wealth by merely forecasting market movements is more than they can bear and so they go at it, not until they win, but until they lose, and lose big. The bottom line is that the market is random and no amount of winning is going to change that. It is the market and not the investor that will determine investor outcome.

Look at the illustration on the next page that charts the S&P 500 returns from 1900. You will see periods of volatility, but for the investor that buys and holds onto shares, a record of unstoppable growth. **But let me point out: The only way to obtain a result similar to the overall result of the long run S&P 500, as shown in the chart, is to buy the shares of strong companies, in monthly increments, and refrain from selling them.** It's as simple as that. The problem for Wall Street, however, is that you can't make a business out of that. People won't pay others to do what they can do for themselves, at least not for long.

If a knowledgeable Financial Advisor puts a client into a four-position portfolio and never changes it, after a while the client will wonder: *"Why am I paying this Financial Advisor to do nothing?"* The correct answer is: *"To do nothing and to keep me from doing something stupid."* But clients are not so wise, so this is not a viable Wall Street business model. Instead the Wall Street culture is one of constant churning.

The chart below is the aggregate result for millions of trades and not a reasonable expectation for one investor. Looking at this chart is like looking at a Ferrari: you know it can go fast but you have no idea what your individual experience with a Ferrari will be. It's just a chart of what happened on the trading floor.

In looking at charts it is well to remember that just because a stock price advances doesn't mean investors have made money on that stock. The only investors who have profited are those who have hung on, which is a very small minority of investors.

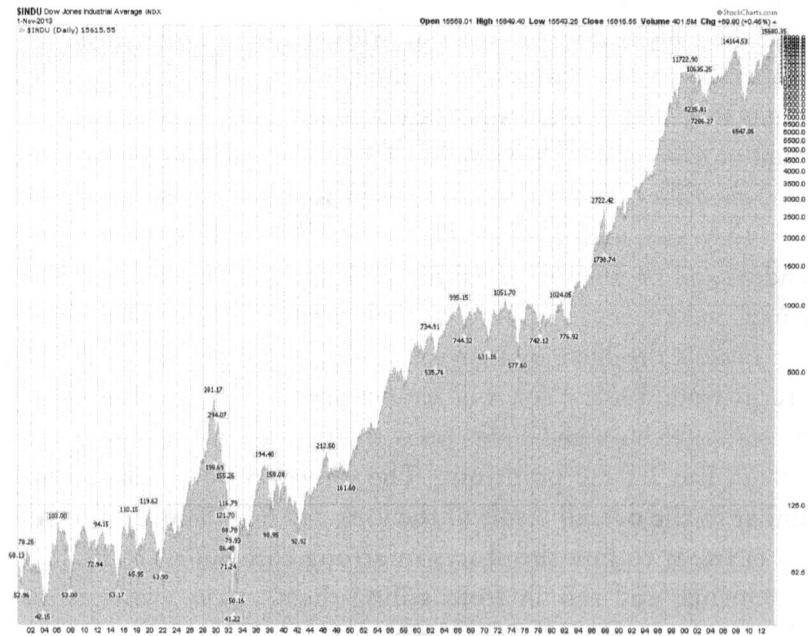

S&P 500 price performance since 1900

Below you will see other indices besides the S&P 500, with results for different time periods displayed in a table. Remember those results are only for those holding periods. Trading in and out does not provide the same result. It's the case of the Ferrari again. The Ferrari is one thing and your relationship to the Ferrari is something quite apart.

Market Indices as of 6/30/2013				
INDEX	12-Mo	3-Year	5-Year	10-Year
T-Bills	0.11	0.11	0.29	1.72
S&P 500 Total Return	20.60	18.43	7.00	7.29
Dow Jones Industrial Av.	22.36	17.07	9.43	8.04
Russell 1000 Growth	17.05	18.66	7.47	7.39
Russell 1000 Value	25.32	18.49	6.67	7.78
Russell Midcap	25.39	19.50	8.27	10.64
Russell Midcap Growth	22.89	19.51	7.61	9.93
Russell Midcap Value	27.64	19.50	8.86	10.91
Russell 2000	24.20	18.65	8.76	9.52
Russell 2000 Growth	23.66	19.93	8.87	9.61
Russell 2000 Value	24.75	17.31	8.59	9.29
MSCI International	17.61	9.95	-0.34	8.35
MSCI Emerging Markets	3.23	3.71	-0.11	14.01
DJ Wilshire Real Estate	8.38	18.28	7.03	10.87

Closed-End Funds & Mutual Funds

Perhaps beginning back in 17th century Holland, when information on companies was not so available, the stock brokers of that day assembled baskets of stocks and sold shares in the baskets instead of the underlying stocks. This would have appealed to investors who didn't have the time to research the companies and make discrete stock selections. And of course, the safety of holding a basket of stocks over a few individual stocks was undeniable. But the real driver was, and is, the fees that may be charged for assembling the basket. So with funds there came fees, and today the fees are often difficult to find.

The first funds were "Closed-End" funds in that the baskets were a fixed size and once all the shares in the basket had been sold, the only way to sell your shares was to find somebody who wanted to buy the very same basket. Of course that is why we have stock exchanges, which are places where people can buy and sell shares. Since having a gazillion people milling around trying to find a "counter-party" to their trade would be so confusing (imagine Grand Central Station at rush-hour), market-makers were designated to trade in specific issues; to add more order, traders also had to be registered.

So if somebody wanted to buy and sell shares, they had to find a trader who would trade for them. That system survives to this day in brokerage firms that are authorized to trade on the various stock exchanges; depending on which issue you want to trade, your broker will go to the appropriate market-maker. This is so efficient that all trades are executed in seconds from the time they are entered by your broker.

There is no mystery to this and it is all perfectly logical. For example, if you want to buy a car, you don't go to the car factory, you go to a car dealer. And dealers are segmented by brand: Ford dealers, Toyota dealers, VW dealers, and so on. This is the most efficient way to buy and sell a car. So, the same for stocks.

There are many people today who, mostly because they are intimidated by how stocks are bought and sold, just buy mutual funds. But mutual funds need mutual fund managers and mutual fund managers need mutual fund fees. There are also fees associated with buying stocks, but these are commissions for either buying or selling. Once a stock is owned, there are no more fees unless they are sold, in which case there is a sales commission. Mutual funds, on the other hand, may have no transaction cost but will require ongoing management fees.

The big difference, however, between owning stocks and owning funds is that the stock owner usually knows how they are invested and why. They own XYZ stock because they like the company. Mutual fund owners don't know how they are invested, typically buying a fund because it is a well-known brand, like Vanguard, T. Rowe Price,

Franklin-Templeton, Fidelity, etc. Then funds are segmented by company size and a variety of other segmentation variables, like economic sector: financials, industrials, etc.

The first funds were fund baskets, as described earlier, that came to be called "closed-end" funds because once all of the shares in a basket were sold, the only way to buy those same share baskets was to buy them from a fund owner that wanted to sell. Perhaps because of that restriction, mutual funds came into existence to sell a particular basket to an unlimited supply of buyers. When there are no more shares to sell, new shares are created and populated with newly-purchased shares of the companies in the fund.

This gave rise to marketing to a larger audience, and to give some pizzazz to that effort, fund "Money-Managers" were added to manage the fund. So while closed-end funds never change, mutual funds are changed all the time, giving rise to the expression of "actively-managed" versus closed-end funds that are "passive." To get an idea how active the management is, most funds have an annual turnover of close to 100%. That's right. The fund is unrecognizable a year after purchase except for the fanciful names they are given: New York Venture Fund, Magellan Fund, New Horizons, etc.

It should be noted here that "Wall Street" is a very dynamic place, always chasing the "latest & greatest," to earn fees, of course. At one time an investor wishing to use an easy diversification tool simply turned to mutual funds. Gradually mutual fund fees began to grow because mutual fund managers noticed that nobody paid attention to the fees, people only cared about performance; also, fees were hidden in the performance figures. For example, a fund having an annual return of 9% actually had a return of 10½% before fees, but investors only looked at the return figures.

John Bogle Spoils All the Fun

Then along came John Bogle and spoiled all the fun. John observed that mutual funds did not outperform the indices they were benchmarked against and that an investor was better off just buying the index and skipping most of the fee. An index is a fixed basket of stocks that is priced continuously, like stock, but intended to measure market action on a particular market segment. Mutual funds typically disclose what index they are trying to emulate the performance of.

Then there was a period where "active" mutual fund and "passive" index fund management was debated, the theory being that "active" management in at least the fast-changing small-cap growth sector was a good idea. But Wall Street being Wall Street, there then was a proliferation of actively-managed "index" funds but with the smaller fees of traditional index funds.

The theory is that index funds don't need expensive money-managers so fees are lower. But the big advantage of index funds, or "ETFs" (Exchange Traded Funds) as they are sometimes called, is that they are labeled for the business sector they track. Mutual funds, on the other hand, are given fanciful names to attract investors, but the names give little clue as to how the funds are invested. For example, a very popular mutual fund is Davis New York Venture Fund, but the fund is not a venture fund at all and is benchmarked or mimics the S&P 500.

As mentioned earlier, the Morningstar style-box matrix was developed for mutual funds. Most people who are not connected with the investment or financial services business sector don't know where to turn for help, so they gradually adopt the idea of investing in mutual funds, which are very large baskets of multiple stocks, in the belief that mutual fund investing does not require a great deal of specialized knowledge and is "safe" because it is unlikely that 100 or more companies in a single mutual fund could go bankrupt at the same time. This is very logical and makes a good argument, but neglects entirely why people invest in the first place: to grow their wages at a rate that beats inflation. Risk is certainly inherent in investment, but there should be some assessment made of risk and not just the knee-jerk reaction that more stocks reduce risk.

First of all, loss is loss and it doesn't matter whether the loss is produced by a company going bankrupt or several companies in a portfolio suffering long-term declines to their businesses. In either case a loss is sustained. At the same time, the more likely cause of losses is likely to be business-cycle expansions and contractions that have uneven effects over a portfolio of stocks.

The idea of a portfolio is to provide for economic swings in advance by using an array of stocks in varying degrees of cyclicality to the business cycle and other economic upsets. Portfolio theory calls for selecting an array of stocks that have differing sensitivities to differing causes of market expansion and contraction. Such a portfolio would be expected to always show returns arrayed in a Ferris Wheel-like pattern with biggest gainers at the top, smallest gainers, or even losers, at the bottom and the rest taking up interim positions around the two sides. The idea is that with business-cycle shifts, the various positions will shift as each comes into a business cycle for which it is particularly suited. By using such a portfolio strategy, the overall portfolio results would be positioned to exploit market expansion while protecting during market contractions. So that is portfolio theory and you don't need more than say 25 stocks to reduce risk down to 4%, while remaining exposed to all the opportunity the market offers.

But even this prescription is overblown, because the likelihood of stocks like Exxon-Mobil and McDonald's going out of business is very low. So why would you want to add lesser-performing stocks to a portfolio of obvious winners when the likelihood of bankruptcy is practically non-existent?

As stated above, mutual fund theory is that if you invest in enough different positions you will almost certainly have a well-diversified portfolio. This is misleading. First of all, funds are often comprised of companies in a single Morningstar style-box, so that would cover only a narrow portion of the business cycle. While professional

Financial Advisors fill all nine boxes, non-professionals may not have the training to do that and adding stocks doesn't necessarily add value – at some point more stocks just degrade portfolio performance.

Mutual funds also usually contain so many positions that in protecting the downside, the upside is restrained. For example, the S&P 500 is made up of 500 stocks, and since the average is the middle value derived from all the stocks, it only stands to reason that half of the stocks did worse than the average and the other half did better.

That is how the average is arrived at. Then the question is: how difficult is it to find the top performers in the 500 stocks? It sounds difficult, but it isn't.

The top performers are companies you know. If new investors put together a list of stocks they wanted to own, the list would be heavily represented by the top performers because they are the well-known companies – well-known because they are successful and have become household brands, and therefore they are known even to beginning investors.

To further illustrate the drag on performance by too large a list of portfolio constituents, let us say that we can do what could be called "bird's eye" investing and invest in countries rather than companies. There would inevitably be mutual funds that offered positions in every country on earth, and other mutual funds that would offer narrower selections like, say Western Hemisphere, or Asia, or even regions like South America or Europe. But looking at all the countries of the world, we can make some pretty good calculations.

We might decide that Germany is a better bet than Zimbabwe, a country that is being ruled by a despot that has driven his country into poverty while enriching himself. The same thing happened in Congo by another despot who even renamed the country Zaire. Given the global landscape, one could safely and easily select Germany or countries like the U.S., Canada, France, United Kingdom, etc., and select out Zimbabwe and Zaire and countries that are an obvious liability. Why would you want Zimbabwe and Zaire in a portfolio along with, say, Germany? For safety? So in the case of country investing selecting individual countries might be the safer thing to do, and easy to do.

Stock market investing offers the same opportunities as country investing – there are companies that are manifestly better than others. Investing in these companies rather than a mutual fund of companies is both safer, easier and more profitable – more profitable because the drag from lesser companies is eliminated. So one can look at companies and give them a probable range of performance. For example, examine the illustration of probable outcomes for companies

A, B, C & D and a mutual fund.

The larger, white Minus/Plus band represents all possible outcomes, which is the same band for stocks and mutual funds. The narrower, black band inside represents probable outcomes for that security.

All securities are expected to make a profit, therefore all are in positive territory. But stocks have a wider range of possible outcomes than mutual funds. This is because as you add more companies to a mutual fund, they offset each other's volatility, narrowing the range of possible outcomes. For this reason mutual funds are thought to be safer. But look at the performance penalty and look at the limitation to upside performance by comparing the average for each stock with the average for the mutual fund.

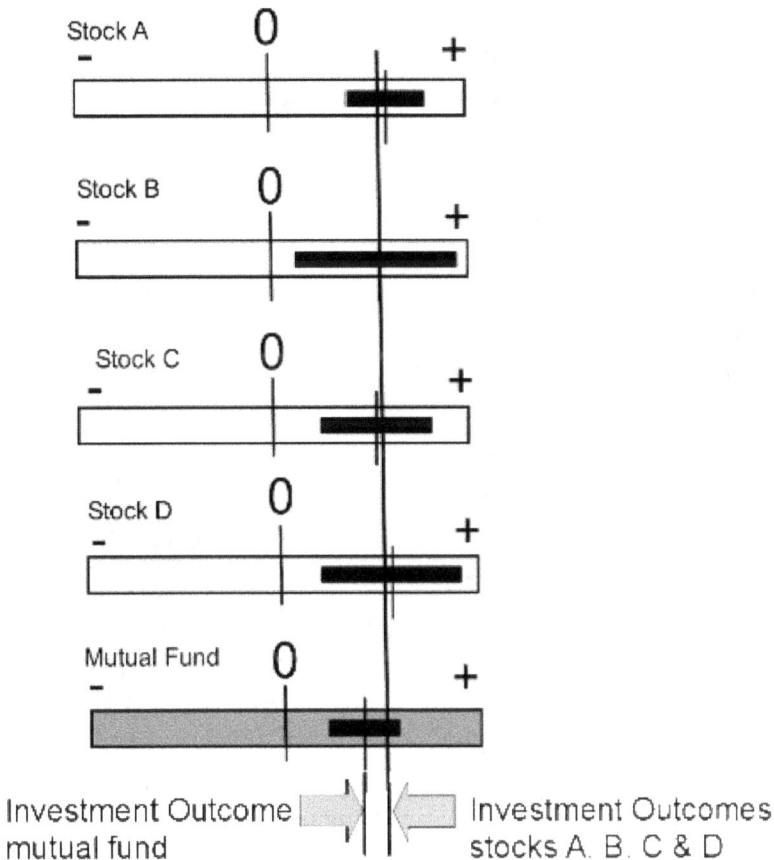

Stock A

Stock B

Stock C

Stock D

Mutual Fund

Investment Outcome mutual fund

Investment Outcomes stocks A. B. C & D

There are just too many stocks in a mutual fund, putting a drag on the outcome of the top performers. And as you can see, the downside is better protected, but at what cost, and what is the cost over a long term like 20 years? The performance penalty is very large. However, for someone trading in and out of stocks chasing returns, the mutual fund may be a good option.

But the best option is to purchase a few well-diversified discrete stocks, hold onto them and ride out the inevitable volatility, allowing those stocks to, over time, deliver their expected returns. And just as it is possible to select-in countries like Germany and select-out countries like Zimbabwe, so it is possible to select-in perennial corporate champions and select-out stocks that offer little more than diversification promise. Just drawing from the Interbrand top global brands is all the research you need to do to meet your future financial needs. But the best thing to do is invest in companies you know, companies whose products you use on a daily basis, companies like Exxon-Mobil, Procter & Gamble, McDonald's and Amazon.

How Dollar-Cost-Averaging (DCA) boosts return

There are three dimensions to investment in the common stocks of the great global corporations: buying, holding and selling.

If the market is random, then there is no way to buy or sell knowledgeably. The only other dimension there is, is the only one you have control over – holding. You alone can determine the holding period.

Shown below is the same S&P 500 chart shown earlier but with several long holding periods illustrated. If you look closely, you will see that all of the buys were at the worst possible time, at the top of the market. Nevertheless, the outcomes were all very positive, because the one thing the investor could control, holding period, was controlled. So in effect, poor investment decisions, just by holding period, were turned into good investment decisions. And you will notice, the longer the holding period the more irrelevant the timing of the buy becomes. This is passive investment.

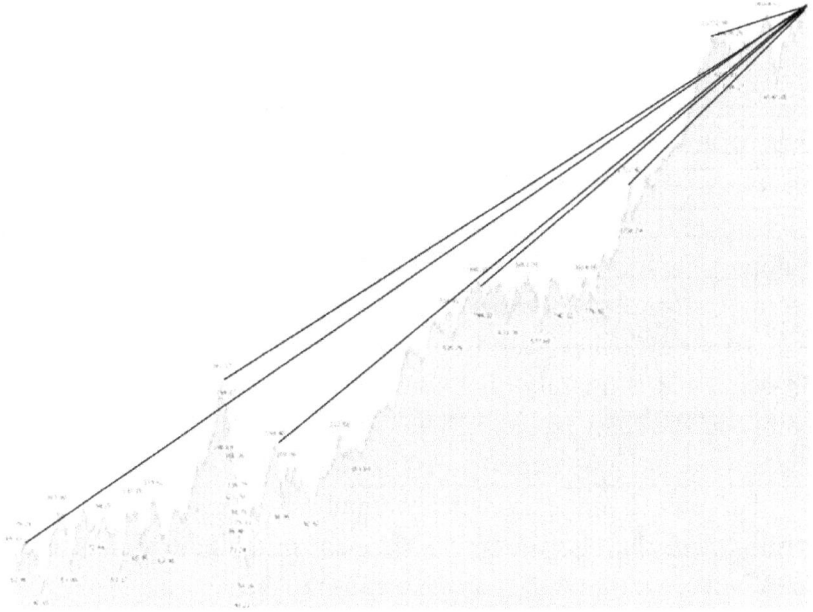

In addition to using the above chart to illustrate success, we can also use the same chart to illustrate losses. And the only way losses can be illustrated is to show multiple sell orders. There is no other way. There is absolutely no way to illustrate losses in this chart without showing stock sales. So there is no other way to say it: **Sales lead to losses!**

Now that you have seen that active selling leads to losses, let us consider another active strategy: active buying. If selling leads to reducing S&P 500 returns, what does active buying do to S&P 500 returns? Look at the chart, and in addition to calculating the return from the worst timing, add in stock buys from all market timing.

There are low points that would have been very good times to buy. And a logical question is: "How did those low points get into the chart?" Those low points mark a point where stock traded hands. That is what the chart is, a record of all the trades in the common stock of 500 of the most prominent corporations trading on U.S. stock exchanges. But the real power of those trades is that it sets a price, a low-price, at which the stock may be purchased. Without sellers to make a new low-point, there can't be any low-points and there can't be any low-point buyers.

Well, who would have purchased stock at those low points? I suggest three types of investors: very lucky ones (if they hang on to their shares) who did a lot of research, very prescient ones (if they hang on to their shares) who did a lot of research, and DCA investors who did no research. And to the lucky and the prescient, I say "Bravo! I hope your luck and prescience hold up," which it won't unless normal statistical phenomena no longer hold.

To the DCA investor, I don't need the qualifier; it will be kept up because it is on auto-pilot. But the point is, that all those low-points on the chart represent points where DCA investors got in at the bottom. DCA investors win 100% of the time!

So, you will immediately see that published fixed holding-period return calculations for the S&P 500, or any other index, do not apply to DCA investors - DCA returns are much higher.

Just calculate the gains from buying fixed dollar amounts monthly. You will see that most of the purchases are at market lows; further consider that those purchases at market lows were for more shares than at market highs. Talk about a Ferrari. DCA is the best a Ferrari can be! There is no other way to say it.

Use DCA to buy stocks of the strongest global corporations and don't sell them! That is the lesson to be learned from looking at long-run charts of the S&P 500 or any other index and the lesson to be learned from reading this book. *"Everything else is commentary,"* to quote a scholar on Torah.

Chapter 7

The Investor

IF A TREE FALLS IN THE forest and no one is around to hear it, does it make any noise? This puzzle was popular when I was in a high school physics class and was proposed as a real brain teaser. I don't know if I ever got the official explanation but my answer is "No." The falling tree sets up vibrations in our ear drums and it is those vibrations we hear as sound. If no ears are there when the tree falls the event is silent. It is quite possible that a physics professor will take issue with my answer, but that is all right, I use the puzzle to get at another point: companies without investors can't survive. Somebody has to keep ploughing more money into companies to keep them going and that somebody is an investor. No ears, no sound; no investors, no companies.

We saw in an earlier chapter that company management does not always succeed, and this goes for employees as well. So you might not be too surprised to find out there are all types of investors in companies and not all of them do that well at it. We have discussed one dimension of that problem, that is, companies to invest in. Not all companies are good investments, but if you stick to the Interbrand top global brands, you should do well. The key word, however, is "stick."

Don't Touch Your Investments

Professor Randall Bartlett teaches finance at Smith College and has two daughters he wants to provide for. But Dr. Bartlett wants to provide more than just money, he wants to provide education in investment and teach his daughters how to be investors. That sounds like a tall order, but he found a way to do it that at least got my attention.

He told each of his daughters that he was going to give each of them $1 million to retire on. Here's how he is going to do that on a professor's income. He will open an account for each of his daughters and buy $200 worth of stock every month for each of them. After 40 years at a return of about 9.45%, which is quite a reasonable expectation, they will each have about $1 million in those accounts. Well, what about the training in investment? For that he merely put a rule into place: he will continue to make those monthly deposits until 40 years is up or they make a withdrawal. If a withdrawal is made, the monthly additions come to a halt on that account. The daughter who couldn't wait gets to keep whatever is in the account, but she gets no more. The lesson is: *don't touch those stocks.*

The Power of Compounding

Now why is that hard to do, and why is it so important? We can start that lesson off by illustrating what Albert Einstein called the most powerful force in the universe – compounding. We are going to take $1000 and show how compounding works; we will use 10% interest just to make things easier. We put $1,000 into an account that pays 10% interest. At the start of the second year, we have our original $1,000 plus $100. Let's see what happens after that.

Year	Original Amount	Year 1	Year 2	Year 3	Year 4	Year 5	Year 6
1	$1,000	$100					
2	$1,000		$110				
3	$1,000			$121			
4	$1,000				$133		
5	$1,000					$146	
6	$1,000						$161

You can see that at the end of year six, the return you are getting on your original investment of $1,000 is 16.1%. At the beginning of the tenth year, you are earning 23½% return. At the beginning of the twentieth year you are earning over a 60% return on your original investment. That is why you don't want to touch it and why Dr. Bartlett can give his daughters $1 million each to retire on.

Now there are usually two reasons people touch their stocks: (1) they need the money and (2) they found a better stock to invest in.

Let's take these one at a time. When you spend money on something, you make calculation on the worth of the thing you are buying versus the worth of the money given up to buy it, but that calculation is based on present value. Well, as soon as tomorrow the transaction is in the past, so that calculation is already old. In other words, that thing you are buying has a life and at some point will no longer be useful. We can say that the object has declining value. This is true for most objects. Almost anything you can think about will at some point either wear out or become obsolete. Money on the other hand, as we have shown, has growing value if invested. So when you give up money for an object, you are giving up something that can grow in value for something that will decline in value. The point of purchase is only the point where those two values intersect in time: the value of the object going down and the value of the money going up. So it might make more sense to consider the future value of the money you are giving up for the object you are taking on.

As a general rule, and an easy rule to remember, in the market money doubles every 8 years. In any given 8-year period it may be more or it may be less, but over a very long period of time using the number 8 as a doubling period works pretty well. So when you are contemplating trading your money for an object, you may want to look forward 8 years and compare the value of twice the money for the object. In 8 years you have given up twice the amount of money: is the object still worth it? After 8 years, many purchases have either worn out or have long since been forgotten, and in many cases, judged not to have been as urgent or useful as originally thought.

Supply & Demand in the Stock Market

The other reason you might touch your stocks is to buy a better stock. This is a very common occurrence. What you see below is a traditional supply-and-demand illustration. Suppliers are always trying to sell at higher prices and buyers are always trying to buy at lower prices. At some point they meet and a transaction occurs. The illustration below shows that suppliers will supply product in proportion to the price they can sell at. If the best price they can get is zero, they will supply zero. If suppliers can get $100, in this market they will supply a quantity of 100. But they won't sell 100 because nobody will buy at that price. If they dropped the price to $80 they would sell a couple. Eventually they would find that the most they could sell would be 50 if they priced their product at $50.

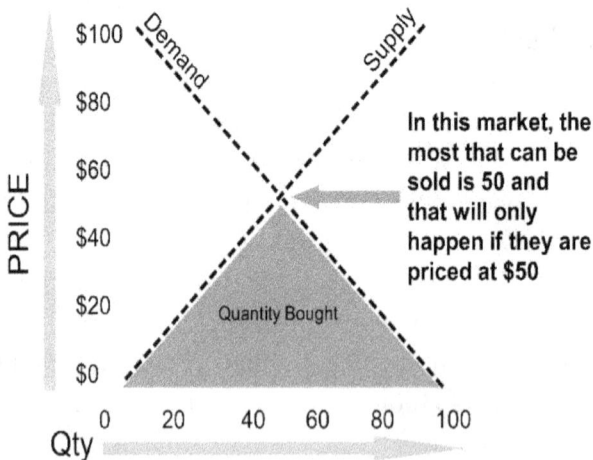

In this market, the most that can be sold is 50 and that will only happen if they are priced at $50

The stock market is like the market pictured above but with one important difference – the quantity demanded always equals the quantity supplied. In most markets there are minimum prices that must be maintained to keep the product sale profitable to incentivize suppliers to keep on supplying. Consequently, with a floor on prices, suppliers must carefully gauge how much product they can sell at a profit and make only that amount.

For example, there are perhaps a dozen auto manufacturers, but millions of automobile buyers whose demand for product is driven by price. The automobile manufacturer cannot easily increase production. Instead, if more cars are needed the manufacturer may have to put up a new factory and decide if they can sell the 100,000 more cars the new factory is capable of producing. The millions of buyers, on the other hand, buy cars one at a time, so for a buyer one more car is a typical demand unit.

Consequently, in the market for goods the supply curve is stepped, so not very sensitive to changed demand. The demand curve, however, is very smooth because if price drops even a little bit, it is likely to result in the sale of at least one more car, maybe two. So the supply/demand behavior in goods markets is not very smooth but rather moves in kind of a jerky fashion. This means stable prices.

The stock market differs from this model in that supply and demand are entirely free of all constraint; they are purchased or sold by the share in any and all quantities. There is never surplus capacity or demand, the price simply adjusts to reconcile all demand with supply. What this means is that price will move freely up and down without any influence from company fundamentals. For example, if there is news on a remarkable invention at a technology company, investors will sell out of all other companies, including food companies, in order to move money into the exciting technology company. Does this mean that the food company whose stock has just slumped is a poor investment? No. In fact it is just on such an "out-of-favor" condition that makes the food company stock a good buy – it is oversold and will gradually return to its prior valuation once the excitement in the technology company subsides.

The Greater Fool Theory

The lesson here is that stock price is very often the first signal an investor has that a stock may be an attractive investment. And the signal will inevitably be that the stock price is rising, that's the news. Now why would someone want to buy a stock that is rising in price, in others words, getting more expensive? This doesn't make sense, but it happens all the time. It is called "chasing return," or "the greater fool theory" – no matter how expensive a stock has become, you can always find a "greater fool" to sell it to. But why is such a self-destructive phenomenon so common? The media. Newspapers, investment websites and magazines must have material to publish, and the most exciting material is in greatest demand. So media suppliers hype whatever news they have, to make it sound more exciting, and that then increases their sales. People read or listen to the "news" and act accordingly.

Some people have what my wife calls FOMO – Fear of Missing Out. Usually this reference is to people who can't stand not getting invited to a birthday party, for example, or learning that a friend went somewhere without them. My wife's classic tale of FOMO was being prevented from attending Billy Springer's birthday party at which a pony had been hired to give the partygoers pony rides. Because she had the measles, my wife, then 12 years old, was unable to attend. She never forgot it and never got over her FOMO from it. I once pointed out to her that we were in Australia once and she got to ride a camel. That's not good enough; she missed Billy Springer's birthday party and there is no making up for that.

So what does this have to do with buying stocks? Everything. Many people feel they must study every stock in the universe before settling on the ones they are going to buy. And if they hear about one they didn't previously know about, they will drop everything to study the newly discovered stock. This is FOMO. The objective of FOMO in stock selection is to know about every stock there is.

The problem with FOMO in stock selection is that in a phrase popular back in the 1950s: "Feasibility fosters fiat." After the atom bomb was developed, it was felt that just having the bomb would lead to its use - Feasibility fosters fiat. Well, this is the case with stock research. Once you start studying a stock, you begin to see that stock apart from all other stocks and soon develop a liking for it and then a preference for it, without any regard for the other stocks around it. Just the investment in time breeds familiarity that leads to preference.

Remember, you can develop a promising storyline for any stock, even for a company that is about to go out of business. The best antidote for this disease, the stock FOMO disease, is to consider that the best way to find investments is by familiarity; the stocks you want are right out in front of you – no research required. You know about these stocks because they are household words, like Microsoft, Walt Disney, General Electric, Volkswagen, etc., etc. They are products you use every day, giving you a front-row seat on how the company is performing.

Indices

This brings us to indexing. Charles Dow (1851-1902), one of the icons of stock market history, once added up the prices of 12 of the most prominent stocks and divided the result by 12, declaring this to be the Dow index. The Dow index was then published regularly, and it gave those following the index a sense of market sentiment – up for euphoria and down for panic. Also, the index advanced with time, giving a measure of overall market movement or appreciation over time.

Soon other actors began creating other indices and today there are a gazillion indices. But for our purposes, the beauty of indices is that they do the stock selection for you. The Dow 12 is today the Dow 30, or what are felt to be (by the Dow indexing Team) the 30 most prominent companies traded on U.S. stock exchanges. And the index is constantly monitored and adjusted, dropping off companies that have fallen and adding companies that have succeeded. In fact, of the original Dow 12, only one stock remains in the index – General Electric (GE).

The most prominent index is the Standard & Poor S&P 500. This is an index comprising 500 of the most prominent companies traded on U.S. stock exchanges. This index is large enough, 500 stocks, to be considered a proxy for the overall market. When someone asks what the market did today, or this week, or this year, the answer is found by looking at the movement of the S&P 500.

There are also indices within indices. For example, if you feel that 500 stocks is too many to tell you very much, there is the High Quality S&P 500 index made up of about 130 stocks drawn from the S&P 500. You may think that investing in this "quality" subset is a no-brainer, but in stock market investing be cautious about "no-brainers" – they are often upended by the facts on the ground. Nevertheless, buying just the S&P 500 index or the High Quality index is a better strategy than those pursued by most of the investment world. And the absolute worst strategy is looking for the "hot stock" of the day.

Stock-Market Sentiment

Be aware that stock market sentiment talks up the winners, and winners show a generally upward stock price trace. The Wall Street media will be shouting out the wonderful news, urging everybody to buy on the way up. This is a mistake, because in its upward movement it will move from an opening position of a bargain, through to reasonably priced, and then enter the euphoria zone where stock price is entirely disconnected from actual corporate performance – P/E may rise from 12 to 50. This happens because all investors hear from the media is that it is a "good" stock without the citation of price – good stock at what price? The investor isn't told. Then when the stock price has inflated to its maximum expansion and there are no more buyers at current price, the stock price begins its inevitable fall and the media chimes in again, now calling it a "bad" stock. This media report brings out the sellers and stock price goes into a steep decline, finally reaching some point below reasonable valuation when the cycle starts all over again.

See illustration on the next page: a plan view and a side view of stock market behavior. The plan view portrays the outward radiation of "news." "News" radiates out in all directions over time; people exposed to the news don't really know when the news was first broadcast, all they know is there is good news on a particular stock and they should buy it.

The illustration on the right reads from right to left. The "news" starts off the cycle. The news comes in when the stock is trading at $20, and the stock quickly climbs to $55 before running out of "buyers-at-any-price." Sentiment on the stock then turns from it being a "good" stock to being a "bad" stock, and everybody heads for the exits.

The Life-Cycle of News

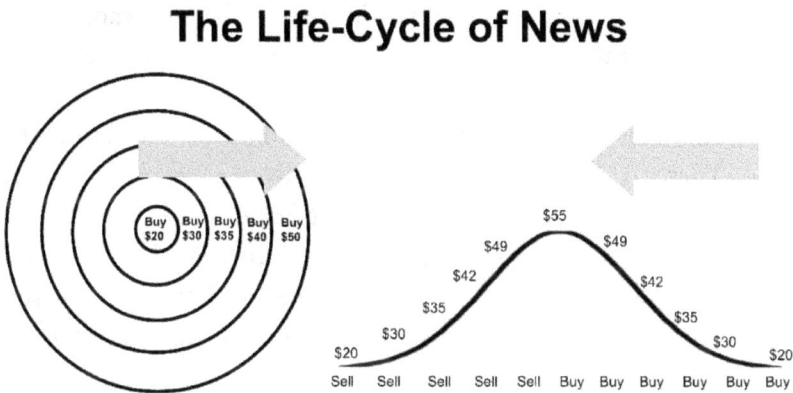

One way to think about stocks is that they live in neighborhoods. You can imagine if your neighbor wins the lottery, how that news will first travel up and down your street, then the next street over and then up and down the cross street and gradually out in kind of a circular pattern like maple syrup being poured over a waffle. It takes a while for the syrup to reach the outer edges.

Stocks have neighborhoods too, made up of the executives at the firm, then employees, then the bankers to the firm and suppliers, then outside auditors and moving out to encompass retirees, then stock analysts charged with reporting on that company. It is only fairly far out that you begin to encounter totally unconnected investors hearing about a particular stock from a Wall Street pundit and/or by reading a "research" report. Reading any report, the reader naturally feels like an insider. That's the magic of the published word, distributed to millions with the intimacy of a closely-held secret – just you and the author, and maybe a few others – at least that is the feeling.

Classic Investment Games

There is story that I first read about taking place in India. A financial wizard was able to gather a large and enthusiastic following for his stock picks. He told half of his audience that a stock would rise in price and the other half that the price would fall. He then divided those who had won into two audiences, again proclaiming a rise to one half and a fall in price to the other half. Taking the winning audience, he again divided it into two, giving one side a rise in price and the other side a fall in price. By this time he had lost most of his audience, but of those who remained, he was able to charge very high fees for his advice.

Wall Street media is not quite this bad, but not too far off the mark. There is another story that reminds me of stock market research. A dairy farmer had a cow that died, and he felt the loss very deeply. His stock broker suggested selling the cow in a lottery. *"How can I sell a dead cow?"* the farmer asked. *"Easy,"* said the stock broker. *"Hold a lottery. After you have sold all the tickets, pick a winning ticket, and call the winner to come and get his cow."* *"But he won't want the cow if it's dead!"* said the farmer. *"Oh, that's all right,"* said the stock broker. *"Just give him his money back."*

The Stock Market is Random

Daniel Kahneman, a researcher interested in investment behavior and a field of study called behavioral economics, was interviewed by German news magazine *Der Spiegel*. Dr. Kahneman described his findings that stockbrokers were not consciously misleading their clients, they truly believed the reports they were reading. Believing these reports, they were able to persuade their clients, with all sincerity, that the reports were true.

Dr. Kahneman went on to describe the stock market as totally random, not something that could be forecast with the level of confidence found in Wall Street "research" reports. Given this input, the best strategy is to just invest in the strongest companies and ignore the Wall Street chatter. Below is a chart showing the S&P 500 price return and total return record since 1928.

The upper line is the "total return" line and includes dividends. The lower line excludes dividends and is the "price-return" line. Now some perspective. The only way you could reproduce the experience of the upper line is if you had bought the S&P 500 index in 1928, reinvested all dividends, and never touched it by either withdrawals or additions. This is the pure result of a one-time investment in the S&P 500 made in 1928.

A better way to think of this graph is to understand that the overall market will rise over time, but not smoothly and certainly not predictably. The real investment world cannot produce this line because people are constantly either taking money out or putting money in, and in putting money in, the only thing that can happen to it is what happens from that day forward up until it is withdrawn. That segment of experience may be very different from the lines in the chart. Also notice that there were periods when the only positive growth came from dividends.

Graphs are very misleading. The only reliable way to obtain return performance data is to enter a starting amount and date and ending amount and date and use a compound interest rate calculator to calculate the rate of return over that discrete period. This will not mimic the actual experience, but will give an overall annualized rate of return for that investment over that period. I use a compound interest rate calculator at www.moneychimp.com.

Charts like the one pictured above have only one reliable use: to illustrate that over time, industry is able to deliver growing value from people getting up every morning to go to work to earn money that will be used in buying what their neighbors produce. That keeps everybody employed. That line will actually be much smoother. The choppy appearance of the graph is just humankind vacillating between optimism and pessimism in their stock market behavior.

The stock market appreciates at about 3½ times the rate of inflation (see chart below), but only if you remain invested in it. If you can't stand the volatility, just close your eyes. This is all the growth you need to finance your future.

YEAR	INFLATION %	S&P 500 %		YEAR	INFLATION %	S&P 500 %
1980	13.5	32.5		1996	3.0	22.9
1981	10.3	-4.9		1997	2.3	33.4
1982	6.2	21.5		1998	1.6	28.6
1983	3.2	22.5		1999	2.2	21.0
1984	4.3	6.3		2000	3.4	-9.11
1985	3.6	31.7		2001	2.8	-11.9
1986	1.9	18.7		2002	1.6	-22.1
1987	3.6	5.3		2003	2.3	28.7
1988	4.1	16.6		2004	2.7	10.9
1989	4.8	31.7		2005	3.4	4.9
1990	5.4	-3.1		2006	3.2	15.8
1991	4.2	30.4		2007	2.8	5.5
1992	3.0	7.6		2008	3.8	-37.2
1993	3.0	10.1		2009	-0.4	27.1
1994	2.6	1.3		2010	1.6	14.3
1995	2.8	37.6		31 Year average	3.63%	12.85%

Chapter 8

ShareBuilder & DRIP Investing

NO MATTER HOW YOU react to the drama unfolding on Wall Street, euphoria on the way up and panic on the way down, there will be drama that will show up as a roller-coaster ride even for the stock prices of the most prominent 500 companies captured in the S&P 500 index, as you have seen. In fact it may be stated quite explicitly, investment in the stock market will produce a roller coaster-like experience complete with butterflies in your stomach as the roller coaster picks up speed on the way down. See chart below for a 43-year history of the S&P 500.

1970	3.95%	1984	6.25%	1998	28.58%
1971	14.31%	1985	31.74%	1999	21.04%
1972	19.02%	1986	18.67%	2000	-9.09%
1973	-14.00%	1987	5.26%	2001	-11.89%
1974	-26.48%	1988	16.61%	2002	-22.10%
1975	37.22%	1989	31.68%	2003	28.69%
1976	23.92%	1990	-3.10%	2004	10.88%
1977	-7.15%	1991	30.46%	2005	4.91%
1978	6.56%	1992	7.64%	2006	15.80%
1979	18.61%	1993	10.08%	2007	5.50%

1980	32.49%	1994	1.32%	2008	-37.00%
1981	-4.89%	1995	37.57%	2009	26.45%
1982	21.55%	1996	22.96%	2010	15.06%
1983	22.55%	1997	33.38%	2011	2.11%
				2012	15.83%

As you look at this stomach-churning volatility, be aware that what you see has been assigned a neutral volatility number of 1. All stocks have a volatility value called beta, derived by calculating the volatility of the individual stock relative to the volatility of the S&P 500. As was described earlier, if the S&P 500 has a volatility beta value of 1, then a stock that goes up twice as much in positive years and declines twice as much in negative years will be assigned a volatility beta of 2. A stock that rises and declines by half of the values in the S&P 500 has a beta value of 0.5.

Given this level of volatility in the stock prices of even the most solid corporate enterprises, it is difficult to imagine that all employees are able to sleep at night not knowing if they will have a job in the morning, even in enterprises that thousands of people depend upon for employment and that millions of people depend upon for products. But surprisingly, almost all get a good night's sleep with no thought at all about losing their jobs. It seems that the turmoil seems to be limited to the stock market and not the companies issuing the stock.

Dollar-Cost Averaging

The natural volatility characteristic of all free markets unrestrained in price movement is viewed by many with great frustration. People buy stocks and then see their value decline. But in fact, volatility can be exploited for the benefit of investors through what is called "Dollar-Cost Averaging," which may have first been espoused by Charles Dow. By purchasing a fixed dollar amount of stock on a fixed schedule, the only variable is stock price and the number of shares acquired – fewer on the way up and more on the way down. That is, few high-priced and many low-priced shares.

In the table below, two purchasing strategies are compared: purchasing a fixed-share amount and purchasing a fixed-dollar amount. If you are buying a fixed-share amount, you are part of the volatility and not screening against it. So you will purchase the same number of shares regardless of market price, and a calculation for the mean cost will be the actual mean of the market, including the volatility.

By metering your share acquisition by fixed-dollar amounts, dollar-cost averaging, you have screened out the most expensive shares and pumped up the population of cheap shares, reducing the overall mean cost of the total number of shares thus acquired. See the table below showing the results after three years. Each column is one year and the last column is the average over three years.

	Early Period $10/share	Middle Period $80/share	Late Period $30/share	Average Share Price
1 share/month	12 shares X $10 = $120	12 shares X $80= $960	12 shares X $30 = $360	$1440/36 = $40/share
$30/month	36 shares X $10 = $360	4.5 shares X $80 = $360	12 shares X $30 = $360	$1080/52.5 = $20.57/share

So by buying a fixed $30 per month, rather than one share per month, dollar-cost averaging results in more shares acquired at almost half the per-share acquisition cost in this illustration. This is a very powerful argument for dollar-cost averaging (DCA).

The Starbucks Story

Let's take a real-life example: Starbucks. In the illustration below you will see a mountain chart of the stock price history of Starbucks common stock (SBUX). The first observation to be made is that viewing charts such as these breeds a level of confidence that comes from having an overview of what happened. One is inclined to point out points at which the stock should have been bought or sold. But remember, the people doing the buying and selling don't have this view, what they see is that performance to the left of the present – they just see history, not future.

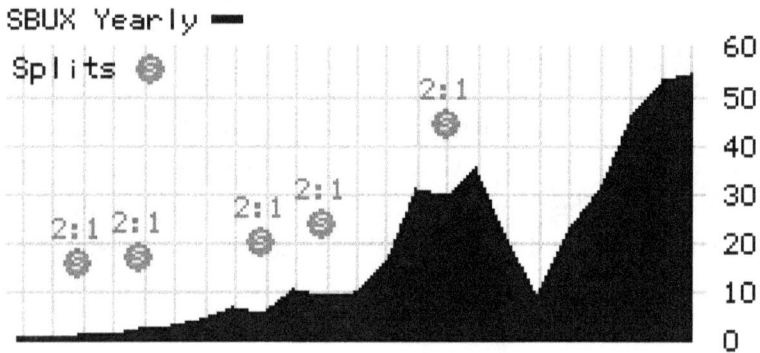

But we can use history to model investment strategies like dollar-cost averaging and draw some lessons. Had a dollar-cost averaging investment strategy been used to acquire shares from the beginning, there would be a collection of shares of many different dollar denominations; but here is the important point: they are all worth, little and big, about $54 each according to the most recent trade pictured in the chart. So that stock takes on the identity and characteristics of the most recent trade, and in fact sheds its birth denomination in your portfolio as soon as you buy it. The identity and denomination of the shares are what the market's most recent trade says they are and have nothing to do with the history of acquiring them – all shares are equal.

Sunk Costs

However, the foregoing neglects another dimension of stock ownership: profit. Some shares obviously will be more profitable than others. Shares purchased in early years will be more profitable than shares purchased later on. Also, notice there will be periods when there will be unprofitable shares, losing shares. There is a deep valley which covers a period when the founder left the company and then returned to restore its fortunes. During this valley period, a number of shares held were at a loss.

Many people do not like holding shares that represent loss because it is an unpleasant reminder of a poor investment made and it poisons the mind for future investment. Sell out the losing shares and start with a clean slate, so the thinking goes. This is a very common practice and derives from the concept of "sunk costs." The concept of sunk costs postulates that money already spent should not inform future decisions because the money, being gone, has no more value. The idea is that if a project is bad, pouring more money into it should not be done unless one approaches it with the same sentiment as if it were being invested in for the first time – the investment either makes sense or it doesn't, and the fact that money has already been invested has no bearing on the reasonableness of the investment thesis at that particular point. For example, before fixing a car that has a long and unhappy repair history, ask yourself, would you buy this car today if you didn't already own it? If the answer is "No," don't make the repair regardless of how much money you have spent so far. Your objective is a car, not this car.

So the concept of sunk cost is very valuable in many of life's decisions and even in stock investing. There are companies that are manifestly deteriorating, and to invest more money in them just because you invested at an earlier time is folly. This appears not to have been the case with Starbucks – it went down and then up. There was never any guarantee that the company would recover, so many who sold all their shares as the company was going down may have had their actions thought of as wise by a preponderance of people with great investment experience. And for them it may have been wise because their profits were turning into losses. This is what happens in many cases in stock market investments, panic selling leading to locking in losses. Some may have repurchased shares in the recovery period and had their faith rewarded with significant profits. But in all of these cases, great emotions were triggered by the volatile stock price movement. And here is a key point: whatever you do, you must believe in it to pull the trigger.

Compare the thoughts surrounding this stock at the start of its recovery by two investors. Investor A sold out and took losses; for that investor, SBUX is a "bad" stock. Investor B did not sell and just kept the remainder of losses in his portfolio, probably by being totally passive and not knowing what the state was of his SBUX investment.

When the recovery is in full swing, investor A cannot admit he made a mistake by selling, and so he stays away from the "bad" stock. Investor B, not knowing there was ever a problem, just enjoys seeing that his SBUX investment is taking off....again!

Obviously, the outcomes from investing in SBUX will be very different for the two investors. Now think: do you think investor A ever succeeds? I speculate that the losses racked up by investor A are other investor B's very nice returns. Of course, the drama would have been missed by the dollar-cost averaging investor B, who just stuck to his monthly purchase program for a stock thesis he liked – premium coffee with no competition – a monopoly on something people absolutely have to have.

Rather than opportunistically buying and selling shares to realize a consequent profit, dollar-cost averaging, that is, buying a fixed dollar amount in shares at regular intervals, takes the emotion out. In fact if there is any emotion to it, it is one of satisfaction in periods of stock-price fall (valleys) so that a greater number of shares may be acquired. In this view, it is not so much the profit of the share holdings that counts, but rather the overall accumulation – how many shares do I own and what is their average cost basis? Regardless of the company's fortunes, having many shares is always better than having fewer shares.

So looking again at the stock price chart for Starbucks, you can get a sense of the relative fortunes of the opportunistic investors and the DCA (dollar-cost averaging) investors. It is possible that some opportunistic investors did very well, but the odds are against such an outcome. For one thing, opportunistic investors must have a steady stream of information to form a view of an investment and such a flow of information is preponderantly in arrears, that is, it reports history as news or rather, forecasts of future price movement. How can the future be predicted? It may be predicted, but that is all it is, a prediction, and it does not have the force of fact, as history does.

Looking at the mountain chart of Starbucks stock it is easy to imagine a steady stream of information, promoting buying on the way up and selling on the way down and buying on the way back up again. This is opposite to the sentiment of DCA investors, slowing their buying on the way up and accelerating their buying on the way down. This is exactly the opposite of what they are "supposed to do." So, a big lesson: be a contrarian. If you are a DCA investor, you won't even have to think about it, your investment program does it for you – you are a Contrarian.

In order to act, you must have information. DCA investors in Starbucks had the information that Starbucks was the innovative prestige leader in coffee retailing. No one else retails coffee like Starbucks. There was a market for Starbucks coffee which propelled the company into a national if not global business. Coffee is something everyone has to have. You can't ask for a better product to invest in, but you need somebody exploiting the need for coffee – Starbucks was doing it. So for DCA investors, "Starbucks does coffee better than anyone else" is the information.

For non-DCA investors the information is whatever comes out of the Wall Street media mill – buy on the way up and sell on the way down. So that is what non-DCA investors do, buy on the way up and sell on the way down. Well, looking at the Starbucks stock price history, you can understand why most investors don't do well.

As the historical price history of the S&P 500 shown at the beginning of this chapter illustrates, stock price changes even for the most solid and oldest companies are pretty volatile. All investors are likely to panic when they see their investments declining with market action, but investments in well-established corporations are easier to bear because these companies have been through many years of up-and-down, euphoria-to-panic, bipolar market sentiment, and they always survive because they are in businesses that provide products people want to buy. In the meantime, DCA investors have acquired an outsize proportion of cheap shares. So here is an instance when volatility is good, at least for DCA investors.

Now, because people lead busy lives and they might forget to make their regularly scheduled stock purchases, or just as much of a problem, not make those investments because of "emergencies," there are mechanisms to put investment on autopilot – which is the best solution.

CapitalOne ShareBuilder

CapitalOne ShareBuilder is a service that makes regular stock purchases automatically for their account holders who choose this option. And here is why this is a very good idea for DCA investors: trading costs. The standard trade in the industry is 100 shares, which is called a round-lot. Of course, many people buy odd amounts of shares, like 50 shares, or 38 shares if they have a rough dollar amount in mind, or 19¾ shares if they are buying a fixed dollar amount. The cost is for the trade and not by the share, so for the above four trades, 100, 50, 38 and 19¾, the cost of just the trade is the same for all four trades, which is the cost to complete the transaction and make the bookkeeping entry.

Trading costs can vary from anywhere between $7 to $100 per trade. So trading costs are a major concern in buying stock. ShareBuilder offers an automatic investment option where program monthly trades are executed for $3.95. ShareBuilder used to offer a program to execute 12 trades per month for $12, or $1 per trade, but that program has since been closed to new participants. Still, to lock-in program monthly trades for $3.95 is a bargain, and gets you the passive platform that you need to succeed.

Another service, Buy&Hold, also offers low-cost automatic trading. It maintains a website at www.buyandhold.com, with terms very similar to ShareBuilder.

While I don't know how ShareBuilder and Buy & Hold are able to offer this low pricing, I suspect that they enter block trades for each security, a gazillion shares of GE for example, for say even $100 for the single trade, and then distribute the GE shares to those clients entering orders for GE shares. This would drive the trading costs down to just pennies per share. But for the investor, to buy up to 12 stocks monthly, automatically, for just $3.95 per trade per month, is an outstanding value. And once you sign up for this service, you just set it and forget it – the market does the rest, supplying mostly the cheaper shares for your account.

Direct Investment

As good as this is, there are even lower-cost ways to invest using DCA – direct share purchases. Companies need investment to grow and are always issuing stocks and bonds to get money to grow their businesses. The default way to raise money with stocks is to hire an investment bank to sell shares. Because the inflow of money may be very large and propel the company to new riches, investment banks may just purchase a block of shares from the company. The company then has what it wants, the proceeds from the sale of the stock. The investment bank then sells the shares they bought on the open market with a story of great new growth the company will realize with this infusion of money. If investment banks are successful (and they try very hard to be), the stock will be sold at a much higher price than the acquisition cost and investment banks make a large spread on the sale.

Existing stockholders don't like this because the number of shares of stock outstanding is now larger and they see their own ownership proportion decline. Existing stockholders prefer "share buybacks," when companies reacquire shares that have already been issued and sold to the public. Companies do this when they have cash and feel their shares are underpriced in the market. Companies reacquire shares in buybacks when share prices are low; then they have "Treasury shares" available to sell back to the public when share prices rise and they need money.

When companies offer shares to the public for the first time, it is called an IPO, *Initial Public Offering.* When the company sells shares for a share issue that is already in the public domain, it is called a *secondary offering* and is offered with some fanfare. Alternatively, a company may elect to offer shares to the public without an investment bank (broker), in what is sometimes called a "DRIP" program, a *Dividend Re-Investment Program* – DRIP. These plans are also known as *Direct Stock Purchase Plans* – DSPP. Whatever they are called, clients signing up for the service will typically have funds drawn automatically from their checking accounts used to buy the stock of the company they are participating in, directly from the company, and at, typically, no trading charge! That is correct, free trades.

Companies sponsoring direct investment plans may either do it directly, by doing all bookkeeping themselves, or they may engage an intermediary like Computershare to distribute the shares, do the bookkeeping and mail out the statements. The regulatory authorities require that clients receive quarterly statements detailing their stock holdings, which Computershare takes care of for direct purchase plan participants in companies that have engaged them. You can go to the Computershare website, access a list of participating companies and study the offering documents of each company's plan.

Some companies charge for stock purchases while others don't, while still others don't charge and offer a discount to market pricing. Almost all offer automatic dividend reinvestment at no charge.

The author has a direct investment program established with Cincinnati Financial Corporation that was started in August of 2010 with the investment of $25 that purchased .9287 shares. Every month, Cincinnati Financial withdraws $25 from the author's checking account and applies those funds toward the purchase of their stock that also pays dividends. Cincinnati Financial also mails out statements monthly rather than quarterly. The most recent statement for this account, reflecting about 4 years of activity, shows that the last $25 installment only purchased .5156 shares, indicating the share price has appreciated since the account was opened, from $26.92 per share 4 years ago to $48.49 per share 4 years later, a gain of about 16.75% per year, and that does not included dividends. The most recent statement listed a quarterly dividend distribution of $15.05. The last 4 dividend distributions have been: $11.02, $12.85, $14.24, and $15.05. This adds up to $53.16 for the most recent year; since the total accumulation is $1,713.09, the dividend yield works out to about 3.10%. So counting dividends the annual return has been about 20%. This is an outstanding result, all without the slightest effort on my part beyond signing up for the program in the first place and with absolutely no fees or trading costs.

Value vs. Growth

To illustrate the role dividends play in returns on investment, examine the following chart. What you see is a comparison of S&P 500 Total Return and S&P 500

Price Return from September 1987 to September 2011 – 24 years. Now, be a little bit careful because the only difference between the two traces is the way dividends are displayed. In the lower Price Return trace, investors received the same dividends, they just didn't reinvest them. So this is not an argument over whether to invest in dividend-paying stocks, it is an argument in favor of reinvesting dividends.

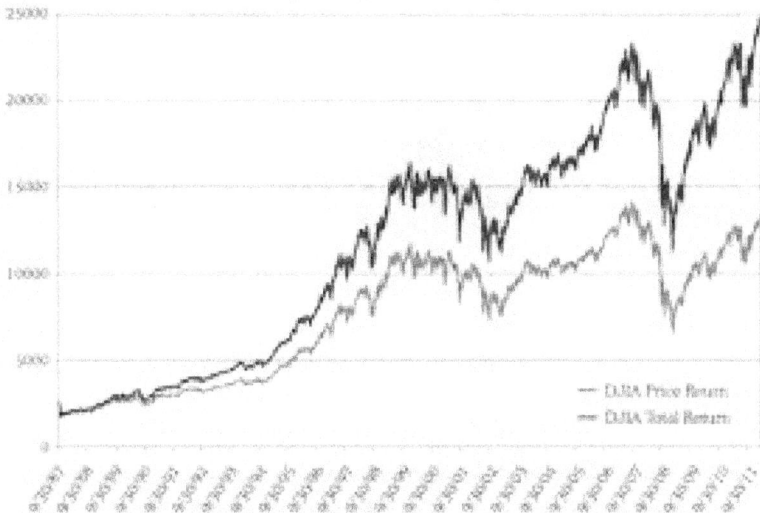

Investors in "growth" stocks don't pay much attention to dividends, but this chart shows why dividends count – but only if they are reinvested.

Now let's look at the "growth" stock experience. Dividend-paying stocks are sometimes called "Value" stocks and pertain to the common stock of companies in the "Cash Cow" phase of their life cycle, able to redirect cash, that otherwise might be used to grow a business, to investors as dividends. In other words, the company has already grown to everything it can be, and profits are better redirected to the investors.

Companies in the growth stage of the life cycle are still growing and need cash to grow. A good example of a growth company is Starbucks. Examine the two charts below to see why. In about 18 months, SBUX stock has appreciated from around $54 to $76 for an approximate annualized price return of 27%. The triangles in the chart on the right are earnings reports, up and down. Stock splits are shown on the chart on the left. Notice on the right chart that Starbucks has begun to pay dividends.

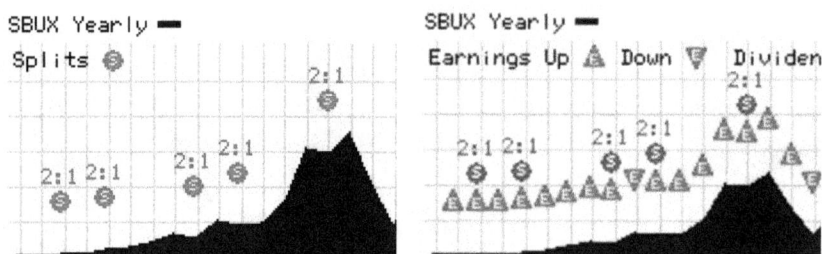

Stock Splits

There is something else in the Starbucks growth stock experience that is worth investigating: stock splits. The theory on stock splits is that investors like to buy stocks that are reasonably priced and may pass up stocks that are out of their "price range," even though the company whose stock has not been split shows a lot of promise. This may be a matter of fashion as more recently, some stocks that may have been split in prior years are today trading at very high prices, forcing investors to buy fractional shares. The idea may perhaps be that high valuations lead investors to believe high value stocks are good stocks. In either case, what ultimately decides stock valuations are company performances. Whether to split or not, from the company's perspective, is mostly fashion.

But from an investor's perspective stock splits take on a very different meaning as they pertain to looking at charts. When a stock is split, say 2 for 1, one share of an $80 stock becomes two shares of a $40 stock. "So what?" one may reasonably ask. It is a question of visibility. When people buy a particular stock they don't look at the overall capitalization of the company to see whether the stock price is too high (overbought) or too low (oversold), they just consider the stock price in the context of recent price history. Some investors might look at the Price/Earnings ratio as a clue to overall valuation, but that does not say very much about whether the stock has never been split in a very long history or been split multiple times over a shorter history, as in the case of Starbucks. Sometimes investors may look at the PEG ratio, which is P/E over growth rate, and that might be a clue as to whether the stock had been split and how many times, but PEG ratios are transient and don't tell the long-term story. So today's investors in SBUX will look at the $79.94 price, see the P/E at 38 and decide to look at a stock chart to get a longer-term perspective.

The chart will incorporate past stock splits by cutting the rise in half every time the stock splits 2 for 1. This will drive down beginning values to near zero for the beginning stock which has experienced the most splits, five for the earliest stock in the case of SBUX, making it appear that the IPO was priced at about 50¢. Starbucks went public in June of 1992 at $17 per share. The first stock split reduced that to $8.50/share. The second split made the first shares priced at $4.25. The third split cut that in half to $2.25. The fourth split made the beginning price $1.125 and the last split made the IPO price equivalent to $0.56. If the stock had never been split, it would be trading at around $2559 with an annual dividend of about $28.15. Many investors would pass up the stock as too expensive, moving on to something else. So that alone might encourage company boards to engage in stock splits, which makes stock splits good for growth stock investors.

Notice that the Starbucks chart on the right includes earnings and that there are only two earnings declines, but the second one was enough to send the stock price to the basement. This is a good illustration of the bifurcation between actual company performance and stock market sentiment expressed in stock price. The best description of stock market sentiment is that it is bipolar, cycling between euphoria and panic. This means that stock price cycles between being too expensive (overbought) and too cheap (oversold).

One might conclude that just going in and buying oversold shares and waiting for the cycle reverse would be one way to beat the market, or beat the S&P 500, but anomalies or mispricing may persist for a very long time. Waiting for something that will certainly happen may sometimes be done with great patience, but waiting for uncertain events to happen takes a degree of patience that is very rare.

Also notice that recently Starbucks has been distributing dividends. Whether an investor is more interested in dividend-paying "Value" stocks or non-dividend-paying "Growth" stocks, acquiring shares by regularized fixed dollar amounts called dollar-cost averaging (DCA) is an optimal strategy, as described earlier. If a DCA strategy had been pursued in acquiring Starbucks stock from the IPO in 1992 up to today, one can look at the stock price behavior after the last split and see that an outsized proportion of cheaper shares would have been acquired as the stock price went through the valley. This particular stock price history is the poster child for DCA investing.

Picking Stocks

But all of this discussion of Starbucks has been in the context of known history, which is a stellar performance after a bad stumble. What seems to have driven stock price is the initial start-up of the company under a visionary coffee entrepreneur named Howard Shultz. After a trip to Italy, where Howard saw the role espresso bars play in Italian culture, he returned to work with a vision of replicating the Italian experience in the U.S.

The Starbucks model worked; stores exploded across the American landscape and Howard sold out, or left the business. Steve Jobs, the magic behind Apple computer, once described people labeled "Managers" as unable to do anything, and he refused to hire them. Well, apparently Howard didn't get the Jobs message – he hired "Managers" to take over his management of Starbucks. Soon the

"Managers" were doing just that, managing, but managing a business in decline.

Businesses will always be in decline because they are surrounded by forces that want to defeat them: competitors winning market share, suppliers wishing to increase their prices, employees wishing to increase wages, landlords wishing to increase rents, customers wishing to pay less, and so on. Incremental managers just respond to the assault and gradually the business loses revenue and profit. So growing businesses, particularly, need management that can "seize the day" and look for new growth areas that are not yet under assault and are therefore profitable. This is how a business is grown; this is the business cycle.

After eight years, Howard Schultz returned to a Starbucks that was in a steep decline and stockholder sell-off. He detected that in the declining Starbucks, customers no longer mattered, it was the cash flow from the business that counted and customers and employees were just a means to that end. Howard turned the company around apparently by just refocusing the company on customer satisfaction and empowering employees to deliver that satisfaction. It worked and Starbucks has been blazing a winning trail ever since.

But the question for investors is: who knew that the business was declining, and why? Why would a knowledgeable investor stay invested in the face of such a decline? Who knew, as the stock price was reaching bottom, that Howard Schultz would return? Who knew that Howard would be able to restore the fortunes of the company? Who knew that the Italian espresso bar model would still work in the U.S.? These are all questions for investors to ponder. And what do you think the Wall Street chatter would have been over this period, and what were the Wall Street "research" reports saying? You can bet that the "research" reports were urging "buy" on the way up and "sell" on the way down, the exact opposite to DCA investing. So how could a dedicated investor have survived through this storm?

You will not be bothered with these questions by investing in the Interbrand top global brands because these are all well-established companies whose fortunes from year to year will not be anywhere close to what Starbucks investors saw in their stock valuation roller-coaster ride. The easy answer is that you must stay the course to win big, but there was no visibility into that; Starbucks might well have failed as a business and taken stockholders' investments with them. And when you look at the Starbucks mountain chart, you can't tell if any investors were in for the whole term or whether the mountain chart shows just the aggregate result of all investors getting in and out as news drove stock price down and then up. This is an important point about charts – the chart shows that an initial investment in Starbucks would have been very profitable, but we don't know that any Starbucks investor ever stayed the course and saw a profit except for Howard Schultz, at least during the period before the recovery.

If there were investors who bought in at the beginning in the IPO stage and stayed the course, they would have had to have had a level of prescience approaching that of Howard Schultz himself. For example, if an investor agreed with Howard that coffee was a core universal product that was not being adequately distributed by the then-existing infrastructure of diners, convenience stores and Dunkin' Donuts, then what would one make of the sudden decline? It looks like the novelty wore off and people returned to getting their coffee at diners, convenience stores and Dunkin' Donuts. And perhaps that is what happened. Howard showed that it was not a novelty by getting his customers back by re-energizing the business even though the product was the same – the coffee didn't change.

What the Starbucks business shows is that there is more to product than just the product, whether it be coffee or cars. There is a product "bundle" that is all the experiences a buyer has besides the experience of the product itself. For Starbucks, it is the experience of ordering from a wide menu of coffees, it is ordering different sizes, it is getting coffee with that iconic logo that confers status upon its users. Starbucks is upscale coffee that confers status and style, on the cheap – the cost of a cup of coffee.

Starbucks is also quality control. You never know what the coffee will be like from a small retailer, while Starbucks puts out the same cup at over 15,000 locations with many open at 5:30am. In short,

Starbucks did to coffee what McDonald's did with the hamburger, distributed it to millions. The difference is that McDonald's has competition – Burger King and a variety of regional brands. Starbucks has no competition, and this was probably the problem with the interim management.

So if Starbucks is so central, why the big dip? Well, while the stock price dipped around say 75%, the business actually dipped only 10%. This was a case typical in the stock market, where euphoria turned to panic, undoubtedly fed by the Wall Street media shouting "sell" all the way down until the stock began to rebound, at which point the media exhortations would have turned to "buy" again.

For the casual investor, which most people are, the best recipe for success is dollar-cost averaging with monthly installments regulated only by the price of the stock. You can do this with a CapitalOne ShareBuilder account, and at some point when the stock goes mainstream, as Starbucks has, you can buy shares direct at Computershare or another direct share purchase portal.

Automating your share purchases using DCA and diversification takes out much of the need for stock and market analysis. Just pick businesses you think are strong, pick the strongest players in those businesses and invest in one through DCA. If you have a portfolio of 4 or 5 such stocks, even if not highly diversified against the business cycle, you will have a foundation upon which you can finance your way through life's great challenges: educating your children and retiring comfortably.

In a diversified portfolio, the Starbucks position may have been 25% of the total and easily tolerated during the period of decline and recovery. That is the objective of a portfolio: to diversify risk and return. If all the portfolio constituents are the same low-risk "value" companies, you may be missing the power of the total market. A portfolio allows you to pursue a broader market experience. But broad portfolios can also dampen returns as the laggards pull down the overall return. Better to choose very thoughtfully and keep the portfolio population small. Your time is limited, so it is better used studying the few companies you are invested in rather than the gazillion companies you are not invested in.

Remember, the objective is growing wealth, and that can be done easily by restricting yourself to the Interbrand 100 best global brands and the best U.S. brands, and the Dow 30. Anything beyond that takes you away from your core objective.

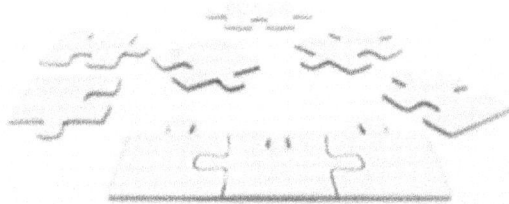

Chapter 9

Portfolio Theory

"DON'T PUT ALL YOUR eggs in one basket!" This often-repeated advice has been around a long time and has particular meaning for investing.

You can think about the trade-off between owning one stock vs. owning four stocks, for example. If you own one stock and it appreciates dramatically you get the full effect. If you owned equal amounts of two stocks, you would only get half the effect. If you owned twenty stocks and one appreciated dramatically, you would hardly notice. But in the stock market no one stock has a monopoly on appreciation, at least not for very long. So the best approach is to pick multiple stocks that are all expected to perform well, which will not dampen appreciation but will dampen depreciation because it is highly unlikely that all four, or ten or twenty, would go bankrupt at the same time. In other words, you are protecting the downside without limiting the upside.

In addition to offering downside protection, assembling a group of stocks offers the opportunity to create a portfolio that offers a variety of opportunities and protections to multiple economic conditions. In assembling a group of stocks some thought is usually given to making selections that are likely to balance each other out. For example, if you selected all manufacturing stocks, the entire group would react in concert to the rise and fall of the business cycle – up in good times and down in bad. A different strategy would be to select stocks that operate in different sectors of the economy and would be expected to behave differently to changing economic conditions, for example adding some food stocks, or non-cyclical stocks to a cyclical portfolio.

Cyclical and Non-Cyclical stocks

Manufacturing stocks as a group do well when the economy is expanding and people want more manufactured goods with the expansion. These stocks are called "cyclical" because they expand and contract with the economy. Cars and appliances and boats are cyclical because in good times people buy more of them. When the economy turns, people stop buying cars, appliances and boats because they either have less money or they are worried about having less money. At such times, "cyclical" stocks will stop growing and may even decline, sometimes dramatically.

But not all stocks are cyclical; there are non-cyclical stocks which are for companies whose products are always in demand regardless of economic conditions, like food stocks and household cleaners. Other non-cyclical stocks are utilities, telephone stocks and pharmaceutical stocks. These are non-cyclical stocks and are sometimes called "defensive" stocks because they defend again down turns in the market.

Not all stocks fit neatly into either the cyclical or non-cyclical category. For example, gasoline is needed all the time but during good times, people might buy more gas to take pleasure trips they refrain from taking in bad times. Also, trucking companies delivering merchandise see their orders decline, so they buy less fuel in down times. So gasoline might be thought of as "semi-cyclical," as would be tires. People can postpone new tire purchases until the economy picks up again.

There are also "counter-cyclical" stocks that may rise in bad times because people are buying lower-cost alternatives. Counter-cyclical might be fast food stocks that cater to people who eat out but choose McDonald's instead of a fancy restaurant. Also people might shop for clothing at Walmart rather than a local clothing store. Discount stores like Family Dollar might do well in a down market.

Then there are stocks driven by other shifts, like casualty insurance stocks driven by weather-related damage claims, and grain and food stocks affected by regional droughts and floods. You never know what the future holds, so creating a portfolio that is diversified across economic sectors offers upside opportunity while at the same time providing downside protection. This is called *portfolio theory* because you are designing a portfolio of stocks to optimize returns under all market conditions.

Harry Markowitz was a graduate student in math at University of Chicago, and apparently decided on a thesis project of analyzing stock portfolio behavior as a math problem after speaking with a stockbroker. Most investors buy and sell on rumor. While stockbrokers like the buying part, they usually lose clients on the selling part. So developing a tool to head off sales was a demonstrated need.

Harry Markowitz then developed the concept of using statistical measures to find stocks that behaved differently under varying market conditions, and espoused the idea of constructing stock portfolios made up of perhaps 15 to 25 uncorrelated stocks. This was 1952 and was greeted by Wall Street as high nirvana because the new tool would give stockbrokers a fig leaf of credibility they could now use on their clients. Harry's finding was labeled Modern Portfolio Theory; it was shouted out across the financial canyons of America and used on unsuspecting American investors who felt they had to have it.

Harry dismissed the Modern Portfolio Theory (MPT) label, saying it was just portfolio theory, there was nothing modern about it. Now, MPT does have a place in the investment world; one place is in the management of the pools of funds found in pensions and foundations.

Pensions and foundations are required to make regularized disbursements from their funds without threatening the health of the fund. If a fixed dollar amount is disbursed monthly, the disbursement seems small when the portfolio is up but may loom very large when the portfolio is down.

A rule of drawing down assets is to go easy when the asset pool is down, leaving a larger pool to recover. Too much draw-down when the asset pool is down and the recovery may be very weak.

For example, study the two tables below that illustrate the recovery of assets due to market action in two ways: the order in which identical market returns occur, early or late; and the impact of drawing down at the rate of 10% versus 7%. The first table illustrates a 10% draw-down with return scenarios reversed, and the second illustrates a 7% draw-down with the same two return scenarios. Examine the total income from the 10% solution and the 7% solution. Total income is the amount withdrawn. In addition, look at the amount of money left over that hasn't been withdrawn.

10%	DECLINES EARLY IN TERM				DECLINES LATE IN TERM		
YR	Return	Principal	Income		Return	Principal	Income
1		$103,216				$103,216	
2	-14.00%	$88,765	$8876		22.50%	$126,491	$12,649
3	-26.48%	$58,734	$5873		21.55%	$138,375	$13,837
4	37.22%	$72,537	$7253		-4.89%	$118,448	$11,844
5	23.92%	$80,900	$8090		32.49%	$141,239	$14,123
6	-7.15%	$67,604	$6760		18.61%	$150,773	$15,077
7	6.56%	$64,835	$6483		6.56%	$144,597	$14,459
8	18.61%	$69,212	$6921		-7.15%	$120,833	$12,083
9	32.49%	$85,529	$8552		23.92%	$134,763	$13,476
10	-4.89%	$70,359	$7035		37.22%	$166,431	$16,643
11	21.55%	$74,874	$7487		-26.48%	$110,124	$11,012
12	22.55%	$76,971	$7697		-14.00%	$85,236	$8523
13	10.88%	$69,274	$6927		10.88%	$76,713	$7671
14	4.91%	$65,408	$6540		4.91%	$72,431	$7243
15	15.80%	$68,169	$6816		15.80%	$75,488	$7548
16	5.50%	$64,727	$6472		5.50%	$71,677	$7167
17	-37.00%	$36,701	$3670		-37.00%	$40,641	$4064
18	26.45%	$41,767	$4176		26.45%	$46,252	$4625
19	15.06%	$43,253	$4325		15.06%	$47, 896	$4789
20	2.11%	$39,749	$3974		2.11%	$44,017	$4401
21	15.83%	$41,438	$4143		15.83%	$45,887	$4588
		$37,295				$41,299	
	TOTAL INCOME		$119,771		TOTAL INCOME		$195,822

Notice the dramatic difference in total income attributable to nothing more than the order in which the identical returns are presented. Negative market action during early years has a devastating effect on asset pools. Of course, there is no defense against market declines other than to meter withdrawals more conservatively.

Now examine the table below, which uses an identical return scenario but makes only one change: it reduces withdrawal rate from 10% to 7%. Look at the difference in total income and the great increase in money remaining in the asset pool.

7%	DECLINES EARLY IN TERM				DECLINES LATE IN TERM		
YR	Return	Principal	Income		Return	Principal	Income
1		$103,216				$103,216	
2	-14.00%	$88,765	$6213		22.50%	$126,491	$8854
3	-26.48%	$61,517	$4306		21.55%	$142,987	$10,009
4	37.22%	$78,504	$5495		-4.89%	$126,475	$8853
5	23.92%	$90,472	$6333		32.49%	$155,837	$10,908
6	-7.15%	$84,139	$5889		18.61%	$171,900	$12,033
7	6.56%	$83,383	$5836		6.56%	$170,354	$11,924
8	18.61%	$91,978	$6438		-7.15%	$158,430	$11,090
9	32.49%	$113,331	$7933		23.92%	$182,583	$12,780
10	-4.89%	$100,244	$7017		37.22%	$233,003	$16,310
11	21.55%	$113,317	$7932		-26.48%	$161,479	$11,303
12	22.55%	$129,149	$9040		-14.00%	$129,151	$9040
13	10.88%	$133,176	$9322		10.88%	$133,170	$9322
14	4.91%	$129,935	$9095		4.91%	$129,928	$9095
15	15.80%	$139,932	$9795		15.80%	$139,924	$9794
16	5.50%	$137,294	$9610		5.50%	$130,130	$9109
17	-37.00%	$80,440	$5630		-37.00%	$121,021	$8471
18	26.45%	$94,597	$6621		26.45%	$142,319	$9962
19	15.06%	$101,225	$7085		15.06%	$152,289	$10,660
20	2.11%	$96,126	$6728		2.11%	$141,629	$9914
21	15.83%	$103,549	$7248		15.83%	$152,565	$10,679
		$96,301				$141,886	
	TOTAL INCOME		$143,566		TOTAL INCOME		$210,110

"What is going on?" you may wonder. Taking out less money results in more money? That doesn't make sense. It makes sense when you understand that the money not taken out has a chance to grow in the market and the more money left in to grow, the more money there is available for total withdrawal.

This is why Portfolio Theory makes a contribution to asset pools that are being drawn down: more is left to work in the market. For example, the returns shown are for the S&P 500 with a beta of 1. Portfolio Theory calls for constructing a low-beta portfolio so that the dramatic declines of say -37.00% are eliminated. The dramatic advances of 37.22% are also eliminated, but what portfolio theory seeks to do is optimize total income by keeping more money at work in the market by reducing volatility.

What has been illustrated is traditional portfolio theory, presented to prevent the reader from being blindsided by someone, like a financial advisor, citing portfolio theory that must be mastered to invest successfully. Portfolio theory is optimal for endowments and pensions that are required to produce regular income – they must reduce volatility for the reasons illustrated. But it has already been shown that for asset pools that are not being drawn down, volatility is a good thing and offers the investor opportunity to buy the same shares at lower cost during market lows using Dollar-Cost-Averaging. So volatility is a good thing for growing asset pools, and portfolio theory is for managing asset pools that must produce an income. These are two very different objectives: growth vs. income.

But portfolio theory is often confused with another Wall Street prescription: *"Don't put all your eggs in one basket."* This of course is very powerful imagery as no one would want to lose all their eggs. This would be a huge loss for someone who is getting breakfast together for a family. But once you examine this statement beyond the imagery you have to ask yourself: "How often are defective baskets the cause of losing eggs?" The fact is that in reality, people whose task it is to gather eggs inevitably do it with one basket, and it works just fine, all of the time.

The problem with using one basket is not the safety of the eggs, but the well-being of the basket makers. And if there are not basket makers, well then, how are the eggs going to be gathered? This is the conundrum that gets solved by everybody agreeing that the more baskets there are, the better. It is a convention generally agreed upon to guarantee a never-ending safe supply of eggs for the breakfast table.

In investment there is a similar convention – acquire multiple stocks because if you buy only one and it goes out of business, your loss is total. This is true, but just like the eggs, the failure rate of companies is about the same as the failure rate of egg baskets – it is very rare and there is plenty of warning long before the failure occurs.

In the meantime, people subscribing to the multiple stock advice buy into the idea of heading off failure by buying and selling stock. And when you get the general population trading in and out of stocks, mostly on rumor, you get what is called *liquidity*. This is the term used that describes the active market for buying and selling stock that allows any issue to be purchased or sold almost instantaneously. The importance of this is that people are never holding money away from the market for fear they will be unable to get back to their cash position because they can't sell their stock. Since the market is so liquid, it attracts the maximum amount of capital, and investors have the convenience of cashing out anytime they want and for any reason – they just want their money. So liquidity is crucial.

Liquidity also means that any new company that has a reasonable chance of succeeding can get financed because they know if they have a good story, enough investors will sell some of their holdings and buy the new company's stock in hopes of realizing the greater return gained from investing in newer and faster-growing companies. In a typical year, 200 new companies are brought to market. There are also "de-listings" or companies removed from trading, often by being acquired by larger companies but occasionally by just falling below liquidity thresholds for lack of public interest. In this way, the stock exchanges try to prevent investor loss in issues that are not actively traded. They are removed from the exchange and stock in these companies cannot be purchased by the public, for their own protection.

Liquidity is a wonderful thing, but it should not be confused with sound investment practice for asset growth. For example, is an investor better off investing in only one stock, say Exxon-Mobil, or a portfolio of stocks that are all recent IPOs (Initial Public Offerings)? The obvious answer is that Exxon-Mobil, having been around for many years and crucial to the lives of motorists around the world trying to get to work every day, is a very safe investment, and much safer than a basket of IPOs.

The lesson is to not blindly buy a number of companies because somebody said to you: "Don't put all of your eggs in one basket." Let's just say that Exxon-Mobil is a heck of a basket and nobody ever got hurt buying and holding Exxon-Mobil stock, while millions of people have lost significant amounts of money chasing returns in the stock tip of the day. For your own well-being, dismiss the idea that all stocks are about to go bankrupt; for maximum growth, invest in only a few very strong companies.

The best approach is to limit your portfolio to perhaps four stocks and then select them very thoughtfully. Portfolio theory was always intended to reduce volatility, equating volatility with risk, because it caused preemptive selling – that is the risk. Or as one wag once put it: *"Risk is between the ears of the investor."*

But DCA investors don't have that risk. In fact, DCA investors are better served by volatility because they acquire more cheap shares. So let's not confuse portfolio theory with good investment practice. The purpose of investment is to build wealth, whereas portfolio theory seeks to limit volatility – two very different objectives.

So, if all investment advice had to be condensed into one sentence, it would be:

"Invest in what you know."

This point cannot be over-emphasized. The Wall Street community wants the investing public to think that there is some dark secret to successful investment, and most people are fooled into thinking that they need a broker to invest. People do need a broker to buy stock, but buying stock, any stock, is not necessarily investment.

There is also another dimension to investment – time. When an investor starts out investing, the asset pool is small and the concern need not be safety – there is little to preserve. The beginning investor has far to go. And one doesn't spur growth in widely diversified portfolios, or mutual funds; one spurs growth by narrower, more concentrated portfolios – portfolios concentrated on growth. As time passes and the asset pool becomes significant, then some attention to preservation may dictate a wider portfolio. But a wider portfolio will always mean greater transaction costs.

Investment is the thoughtful contemplation of discrete company prospects based on the markets they are serving and the prospects for those markets: are they growing or declining? One would want to know how the companies are performing relative to competitors. Is the company a brand leader? Is the company innovative? So all of these characteristics are important to understand; one of the problems with portfolio theory is that it considers companies only from the perspective of its behavior in a large population of stocks. Corporate identity is lost to consideration of a paranoia-laden concern for safety in a U.S. market that has been around in continuous operation since 1792.

The best antidote is to invest in what you know because if you know how you are invested, you are immune to market chatter meant to produce euphoria and panic that sells information to people who don't know how they are invested. The only information you need is what you see every day and what is reported in your daily newspaper.

Business Sectors

Nevertheless, investors should know what the market landscape looks like so that they can know what all the shouting is about. A good start to identifying what to know is to start out by examining business sectors. There are a variety of sources on cyclicality in stocks, but the table below seems to be a compilation of the literature on the subject. Business sectors are identified as either "cyclical" or "non-cyclical" whereas in fact, businesses exist in an analog range of cyclicality, from non-cyclical to highly-cyclical.

CYCLICAL	NON-CYCLICAL
Financials	Defense
Consumer Discretionary	Consumer Staples
Technology	Health Care
Industrials	Energy
Materials	Telecom

According to the table there are 10 sectors, so a portfolio made up of 10 stocks, one from each sector, might be a good portfolio strategy if it weren't for transaction costs. Remember, it costs the same to buy 1 share as 100 shares, so DCA investing in multiple small share purchases is discouraged. The investor has the tradeoff of buying many shares in a few stocks or a few shares in many stocks. Better to restrict the population of stocks to a few you know and bulk up on just those issues.

The business cycle has an influence on the availability of loans for borrowing to grow a business. During the expansion phase of the business cycle, banks are anxious to lend money and lower rates to draw in more borrowers. In fact, it may be low rates that prompt the expansion. Smaller companies are generally faster-growing and are short on cash, which is diverted to growing the business. So smaller, faster-growing companies are users of cash and are therefore likely to thrive in a low-interest expansionary economy. When the cycle turns, banks reduce borrowing by raising rates, generally freezing out smaller companies; then larger companies, that may have a lot of cash on hand, thrive.

Stock price appreciation is the result of actual company performance and investor sentiment, so in good times, investors bid up smaller "Growth" companies. When the economy turns, investors abandon the smaller companies and move their money to large "Value" companies in what is sometimes called a "flight to quality." During such times, small company stock price slumps and large company stock price advances. This is the business cycle magnified by stock price gyration.

There is an investment style called "Contrarian" that calls for always buying out-of-favor stocks, or moving against the market. This style is also called "Dow Theory." But since one never knows the schedule of the cycle, dollar-cost averaging is the only reliable way to be a Contrarian or a Dow Theory investor.

Morningstar Style-Box Matrix

An organization named Morningstar has captured company diversification by growth and value in their well-known style-box matrix shown below.

The Morningstar style-box matrix is a very useful and popular diversification tool. As you can see by examining the matrix, the vertical coordinate is size by capitalization (stock price X shares of stock outstanding) with larger capitalization companies at the top. The horizontal coordinate is growth rate, with slower-growing "Value" companies on the left and faster-growing "Growth" companies on the right.

In the illustration, you can see that the "style-boxes" incorporate the broad market index, which is all companies of all sizes and life cycles that are available on U.S. stock exchanges. The two most prominent exchanges are the New York Stock Exchange (NYSE), sometimes called the "Big Board," where "Value" companies may be found, and NASDAQ, where "Growth" companies usually trade.

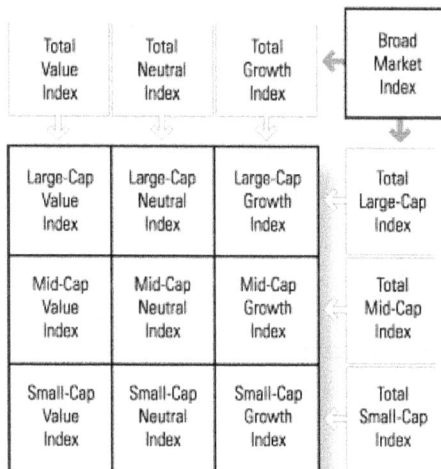

Total Value Index	Total Neutral Index	Total Growth Index	Broad Market Index
Large-Cap Value Index	Large-Cap Neutral Index	Large-Cap Growth Index	Total Large-Cap Index
Mid-Cap Value Index	Mid-Cap Neutral Index	Mid-Cap Growth Index	Total Mid-Cap Index
Small-Cap Value Index	Small-Cap Neutral Index	Small-Cap Growth Index	Total Small-Cap Index

Morningstar® Style Index Family

It might help to identify a few well-known companies in relation to the Morningstar matrix. Beginning with the upper-left style box labeled "Large-Cap

Value," you can think of a company like Procter & Gamble (PG). PG is known for dominating the consumer staples business sector with household cleaners and other household commodities that America shops for at the local grocery store. Because the need for household products doesn't change much from year to year or with the business cycle, it is a slower-growing sector and is able to direct excess cash flow to owners (stockholders) in the form of dividends, thus the term "Value" connected with this column.

Moving down the value column, you have companies smaller than PG; in the mid-cap space you may have utilities that are slow-growing because they are dependent on selling electricity, and population growth driving electricity demand growth is just not fast-moving. Utilities are known as stable dividend-payers; investors like them in their portfolios for the stability and reliable cash flow in the form of dividend distributions.

The bottom style-box represents small-cap companies in the "Value" column; this may be some smaller retailers like Family Dollar and also some publicly-traded partnerships, which we have not discussed.

Unlike major corporations, "C" corporations, that can grow in any sector offering growth and opportunity, publicly-traded partnerships operate in narrow sectors that exploit a fixed asset like real estate, real estate mortgages, small company financing, tankers, petroleum and natural-gas pipelines, forests and so on.

Publicly-traded partnerships (PTP) pay exceptionally high dividends and are generally not as highly correlated to the business cycle as other stocks, so are favored for their diversification value. However, this makes PTPs more difficult to understand during a financial storm. For example, tanker stocks, like Navios Maritime, earn their revenue by sea transportation that has a business cycle driven by the availability of competing tankers. But tankers have different routes, with each route rising and falling in revenue generation based on conditions other than the business cycle, like the demand for one commodity over another or the widening of the Panama Canal to admit larger ships. In such a case, a fleet of smaller ships will lose the Panama Canal route advantage while fleets having larger ships will now compete in that route. Characteristics like this make PTPs more difficult to select since they don't fit the typical business-cycle model. But for the DCA investor, PTPs make some sense and provide outsize dividends.

The center column in the Morningstar matrix is a side-to-side blending of the value and growth columns, apparently offered as a way to diversify by simply buying mutual funds labeled "blend" which might contain both "Value" and "Growth" companies in that capitalization size. There are three blend categories: "Big-Cap Blend," "Mid-Cap Blend" and "Small-Cap Blend," because the blending is side-to-side only.

The growth column, on the right, contains mutual funds made up of companies that are faster-growing. For the top style-box, "Big-Cap Growth," you may think of General Electric (GE). This may not be a perfect fit, but the point is that GE is constantly acquiring and disposing of businesses based on profitability and growth-rate. GE is looking for high-growth businesses where the GE brand can add value, so in my calculation that makes GE a growth company even though they have been around a long time and they distribute, currently, a 2.80% dividend. Also, GE is a technology company and technology is a growth sector. Another candidate for this big-cap growth style box is Intel (INTC), an obvious technology company.

The next style-box down is mid-cap growth; two more-prominent members of this group are Netflix (NFLX) and Green Mountain Coffee Roasters (GMCR), makers of the Keurig coffee-maker. Both companies are still in a growth stage expected to expand further.

Small-Cap Growth, a Difficult Sector

The bottom right style-box, small-cap growth, is where most of the other companies began their life – even GE was at one time a small-cap growth company.

But companies in this sector are difficult to pick out because it takes more than just being in the right business to survive; these companies must have money to grow and very skillful management to guide them – and then there is competition. Sometimes a company may have all three attributes – good product, plenty of money and good management – but simply gets out-maneuvered by a competitor who has slightly more of each. For example, it wasn't certain early on that the Keurig coffee maker would be the coffee maker of choice, but it gradually beat the competitors in a fierce battle. In this particular coffee-product fight, what was interesting was that Keurig was an unknown going up against well-established brands. Keurig had a good product, good management and, apparently, enough money to keep on fighting. But for an investor, an early selection of Keurig would have been just a wildly speculative guess, and that is not how you make money.

So to fill this sector of your portfolio, you may be better off relying on the experts and selecting a small-cap growth fund, letting the experts track every scrap of news and adjust their selections accordingly. You can enter "small cap growth etf" as a search term in Google and you will quickly get a selection of ETFs (Exchange Traded Funds) which usually track an index like "Small-Cap Growth." The alternative is to rely on GMI ratings of small-capitalization companies to select companies noted for their fiduciary rigor, but GMI ratings are hard to get.

As a caution, the reader should know that most investors are mutual fund investors and they and their financial advisors follow the Morningstar Style-Boxes. The downside of this is that the investors have no idea how they are invested. In addition, they overburden their portfolios with stocks that provide a level of downside protection they don't need while limiting their upside growth.

To focus on discrete companies, a much more sensible approach, examine the Interbrand leading brands and the Dow Jones 30, sometimes called the Dow-Jones Industrial Average (DJIA), made up of the 30 most prominent common stocks in the U.S.

Below is a list of ten of the longest-term members of the DJIA with their dates of admission to the index:

1. GE - 1896
2. Exxon-Mobil – 1928
3. Procter & Gamble - 1932
4. DuPont – 1935
5. United Technologies 1939
6. 3M – 1976
7. IBM – 1979
8. Merck – 1979
9. American Express – 1982
10. Pfizer – 2004

Looking at these 10 constituents of the DJIA, it is difficult to see in them a level of risk that would propel an investor to prefer a mutual fund as a safer source of growth. What the mutual-fund and index-fund industry does is exploit the natural hesitation most people have of developing their own security selection based on their everyday life experiences, feeling that such familiarity is amateurish and unequal to the task of sophisticated security analysis. This is precisely why this book is written. Investment in the companies you know and experience every day is the best way to invest.

In investment, nothing beats familiarity, and the greatest familiarity comes from using a company's products and services and being exposed to their ability to satisfy their markets every day in ways that you can see and touch and experience personally. Making calculations of revenue and profit does not tell you any more than the state of that company's fortunes at that moment in time – it is a snapshot. Investment is not made on snapshots. Investment is the passionate belief that a company possesses products, internal cultural characteristics and management that allow it to be dominant in serving a growing and robust market. If there is competition, all the better to see how your company is performing. You don't need a PhD from MIT in security analysis. You need eyes and ears and a brain to think about what you see and hear, and that is all you need.

ADR, ADS

In the earlier discussion on corporate governance, it was shown that there are variations in corporate governance across cultures, so this is an additional opportunity to diversify. And diversifying across countries adds the dimension of insulating against market upsets that may be centered only in the U.S. economy.

It was also pointed out that many offshore companies fled the U.S. major markets when Sarbanes-Oxley rules placed burdensome reporting standards that would be useful in heading off fraud but had the effect of driving good companies out. But these good companies are still accessible through American Depositary Receipts (ADRs) in the OTC (Over-the-Counter) market.

The OTC market is often thought of as the place where small companies are traded, which is true, but it is also the place where some of the most successful and prestigious off-shore companies fled to after Sarbanes-Oxley. For example, BASF, a German-based global chemical giant with a market capitalization of $106 billion, may only be purchased as an ADR in the OTC market in the United States. Just to compare, two American chemical giants, DuPont and Dow, have capitalizations of around $60 billion, substantially smaller than BASF.

So in developing diversifying strategies, in addition to "Value" and "Growth" and capitalization, it would be good to diversify by country, which is to say, diversifying by culture and corporate governance.

In examining the OTC market for larger capitalization stocks, you are entering a recognizable world populated by offshore companies whose products you are familiar with and use regularly. Some of these offshore companies are Nestle, BMW, Daimler, VW, Michelin, Panasonic, Samsung, and so on. Sony is traded on the NYSE.

One could create a portfolio from just the Dow 30 or reach out to the broader population of the S&P 500 or narrow that down to about 130 stocks in the S&P 500 High-Quality index and include big-cap OTC stocks. Choosing from this population will bias you toward "big-cap value" and away from growth. For growth, look in the tech sector, companies like Intel, Google, Yahoo, possibly even United Technologies, IBM and Amazon.

The typical rule in making allocation decisions is time horizon, how long before the portfolio begins its draw-down phase. The longer the time horizon the more aggressive the portfolio not only can be, but should be. As time passes, one way to smooth out portfolio returns is to increase the number of constituents using cyclicality and other diversifying parameters like offshore, casualty insurance stocks and military stocks. An aggressive long-run portfolio may be as few as four positions in very strong and well-diversified companies, like Procter & Gamble with over 100 brands in almost every country in the world. This is internal diversification, and all the diversification you need in a long-run portfolio.

As the time to start the draw-down in retirement approaches, volatility will become an obstacle rather than an aid and it may be time to widen the portfolio to include perhaps twenty stocks with an emphasis on large-cap dividend paying stocks.

The dividend distribution will not follow the volatility of the stock price or the broader market. The yield will be pretty much unaffected by stock price, and this translates into dividend checks that are growing at three to four times the rate of inflation regardless of what the stock price is doing.

You can check this by going online to an interactive chart like Big Charts. Bring up a high-beta stock and enter a range like ten years and elect to show dividends. The dividends will be shown in quarterly distributions in dollar values. You will then see that while stock price is gyrating all over the place, the dividends just exhibit a smooth appreciation over time, like $1.11 for four quarters then $1.23 for five quarters, then $1.37 for three quarters and then $1.54, etc.

As time passes and you are nearing retirement, you can gradually ramp up from say four stocks to perhaps ten or twenty or more stocks to take out the volatility. But remember, retirement lasts a long time these days and is getting longer. Don't give up the growth just because retirement is approaching – you have plenty of time to go yet.

In the early years, for growth and to keep transaction costs down, use only four carefully selected stocks that perhaps are internally diversified. Even if the four stocks are all cyclical stocks, it doesn't matter because you are not taking money out.

Four cyclical stocks acquired over time using DCA is a growth engine. And don't be overly concerned with which stocks. Many years from now, when you look at the accumulation, it won't much matter which stocks you chose within the Dow 30 or Interbrand 100, what will matter is that you executed an investment plan faithfully over many years.

Chapter 10

Portfolio

MODERN PORTFOLIO THEORY, by aggregating non-correlated assets, is designed to reduce downside volatility so that cash flow out will not threaten the health of the fund with withdrawals at performance lows; but by the same token, volatility to the upside is also reduced, and that is contrary to the objective of aggregating wealth. So Portfolio Theory is for mature asset pools that are approaching the draw-down phase or are being drawn down in retirement. But in earlier years, when building an estate, the only concerns are reliable growth. Not the unreliable growth of a "hot" IPO, but the reliable growth of an Exxon-Mobil or P&G returning 11% over a very long period of time and then driving that return up with dollar-cost averaging.

Now, to focus on the objective of building wealth, we will put portfolio theory aside and consider a four-position starting portfolio producing diversification mainly over time with a spectrum of share prices that will fluctuate, but in a process that favors cheaper shares.

For the first position, I pick Exxon-Mobil. What I like about Exxon-Mobil (XOM) is that it is a very large and successful company operating across the world in a commodity that everybody needs, transportation fuel: gasoline for cars, diesel for trucks and trains, jet fuel for planes and so on. It is hard to imagine a world without these things; owning the stock of one of the strongest players is probably about as safe a stock as you can own and one that provides as good a return as you can expect. A quick look over the past 12 years indicated Exxon-Mobil return at 8½% annual stock-price appreciation plus 2½% in annual dividend yield totaling an average annual return of 11.00%. Of course the actual year-to-year performance was not that smooth but if you are buying and holding, you are only concerned with the end result and not the interim volatility.

And since you really don't have to be too concerned about Exxon-Mobil going bankrupt since it is well diversified across the world with a basic commodity everybody needs every day, an 11.00% return is outstanding. But it is even better than that, because the 11.00% is just for a fixed dollar amount between two points, the beginning and end of a 12-year period. By dollar-cost averaging, you are still getting the end point, but filling in after the beginning points with cheaper shares, loading up on Exxon-Mobil when it is down and reducing acquisition cost during the high periods. With DCA, you can count on an even higher return over time, as has been shown.

Also, I am mostly ambivalent between Exxon-Mobil and Royal Dutch Shell. I think perhaps Royal Dutch Shell may be better situated in the corporate governance dimension, for two reasons: the separation of Board Chairman and CEO and the split oversight of both the Brits and the Dutch. But when you are in this league, these differences may be misleading. On balance, I prefer Shell, but Exxon-Mobil has one huge advantage: it is available not only in a DRIP program, but a Roth IRA DRIP program. Nothing produces more drag on wealth creation than selling out positions. But the next greatest drag on wealth creation is taxes, and Roth IRAs reduce taxes down to a minimum. So that is a very powerful argument for Exxon-Mobil (XOM).

Well, that was fun, but we need three more stocks to make up our 4-stock portfolio. If we are searching for something that is uncorrelated we can think about some correlation factors. The easiest way to do this is to think about stocks that share some factors we don't want to correlate against, like global market and staple commodity that everybody needs. But people need more than gas – what about household cleaners? Even during a depression people buy soap. So we can add Procter & Gamble (PG).

Procter & Gamble, like Exxon-Mobil, is a very large company serving a global market with commodities everybody needs. But unlike Exxon-Mobil, Procter & Gamble has many more products, so it is diversified internally as well as externally across the world. While Exxon-Mobil is almost all fuels for cars, trucks, trains and planes, Procter & Gamble has about 100 brands in such diversified sectors as grooming, beauty, health care, baby & family care and home & fabric care. Twenty-five of the brands generate over $1 billion annually in revenue. Many of the brands are globally recognized iconic brands, like Gillette, Ivory, Pampers, Tampax, Downy, Cascade and Duracell. So in its internal diversification and focus on low-cost commodities, unlike gasoline, P&G is a good uncorrelated second position with respect to Exxon-Mobil.

Well, what else do people buy that would be uncorrelated to gasoline and household staples? How about food? It would be hard to imagine people giving up food so this is a good place to look. According to Interbrand, a good place to look for stocks in the global brand rankings, the top five food brands according to Interbrand are Coca-Cola, McDonald's, Pepsi, Kellogg's and Budweiser, a product of Inbev. Any of these would make an excellent investment, but I like McDonald's because it seems to have dominated the fast-food space for many years against all competitors. Also, the other brands are mainly a more narrow sector, like breakfast for Kellogg's and beer for AB Inbev, or soft drinks for Coca-Cola and Pepsi. McDonald's does breakfast, lunch and dinner with beverages and in about 119 countries. The others would be fine, but I like McDonald's because McDonald's is more differentiated from its competitors. Also, McDonald's offers a DIRECT investment program with a Roth IRA option.

Now we need a fourth stock. What else do people buy? Well, what about a retail stock like Amazon, Walmart or Home Depot? They are well-diversified. Or what about financial services? But people also buy computing and there are two brands there that are recognized globally as having few if any serious competitors: Microsoft and Intel. These are all excellent choices, but the one I select is Amazon. I like Amazon because it seems to be succeeding at its mission of selling everything that can be sold. It is an expensive stock, but with a high growth rate and dollar-cost averaging, we can bring down the average per-share cost.

Below, you will see the resulting four-stock portfolio showing the beta and dividend yield for each position. Professional money managers would take issue with the lack of diversification by capitalization size and just the overall narrowing down to just four positions. But recall, this is not an endowment that needs cash flow but rather a stable growth engine designed to stay ahead of inflation and be a "SWAN" investment for its adopters – SLEEP WELL AT NIGHT.

And there is one other dimension to this portfolio: by using DCA (Dollar-Cost Averaging) over time the portfolio becomes diversified by an often-overlooked but powerful diversification strategy - the accumulation of shares over a wide spectrum of acquisition cost. So when the market tanks, it's not an individual stock that will be down, but only those individual shares in each of your positions that were acquired at market highs.

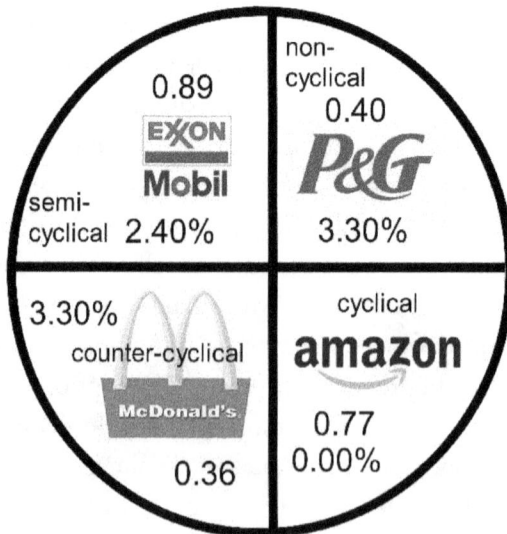

Diversification by Time

When an investor acquires blocks of stock each share is priced identically, which means when the stock is down, the entire position is down. And since many investors acquire their entire portfolios in large blocks, to reduce transaction costs for one reason, the portfolio turns out not be so well-diversified because when the market turns, all stocks are more or less affected in the same way. When the market is down, "diversified" portfolios are down. But by diversifying by time, acquiring shares that differ in acquisition cost, a portfolio is never "down" as a whole, only down in those shares that have a higher acquisition or "cost-basis," which will only be a portion of the portfolio. See illustration below.

Then combining Diversification-by-Time (DBT) with Dollar-Cost-Averaging (DCA) where each stock purchase is only one in a series of equal monthly additions, higher priced shares, at market highs, are limited to a fixed price and become a disproportionately small component of the overall holding. The higher the price, the fewer the shares acquired and the lower the price the greater number of shares are acquired. See in the illustration below that most shares are profitable even in a market downturn, because more shares were acquired at market lows. Low-priced shares far outnumber high-priced shares, thanks to Dollar-Cost-Averaging.

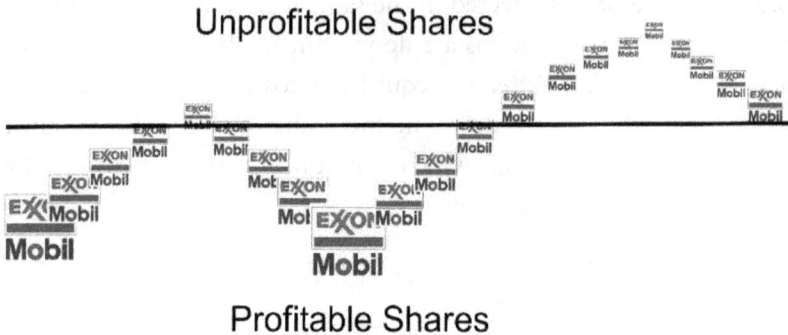

Unprofitable Shares

Profitable Shares

Transaction Costs

The downside of DCA is high transaction costs. Every time you buy stock there is a fee, and the fee is the same whether you buy one share or a hundred shares. This discourages monthly DCA purchases.

It has already been described that much of Wall Street stock advice is designed to enrich the source of the advice rather than the destination of the advice – the investor. Those in the business of serving investors need to be paid for their services, but since really, very little service is required, there should be very little pay. Unfortunately, this is not the case. The business community serving investors is extremely well-paid. The source of the pay is the perception that all of the work required to invest is really necessary and that it is really valuable. This is a ruse. Regularized investments into four stocks forming the above portfolio, described earlier, should be almost without fee.

If you use an account at ShareBuilder or Buy&Hold, you can elect monthly investments for $3.95 per trade, which for amounts of say $100 would be an initial drag of 3.95%. For let's say a monthly investment of $500, the transaction cost goes down to 0.079%, which is not too bad. Or you can avoid almost all of the transaction cost altogether by using a Direct Investment Program (DRIP), buying stock directly from the company though a stock transfer agent like Computershare. This is ideal, but there is a hitch: the custodial fee for managing an IRA account at Computershare is $45 per year. Say you invested $100 per month into a DRIP IRA, at the end of the year you will have accumulated $1200; with an annual custodial fee of $45, the drag during the first year will be 3.75%, which is significant but will decline with every passing year. For example the second year drag will be 1.88%. And the drag will go down from there.

For more on DRIPs go to several websites serving the DRIP investor - www.dripadvice.com is one; www.dripinvestor.com is another; and there are others. If you acquire stock through a DRIP account that is a regular taxable account and not an IRA, there is very little transaction cost and very little drag. One strategy would be to use a DRIP to acquire a $5500 position in a stock and then convert it to a Roth IRA DRIP, which is available for Exxon-Mobil and McDonalds, but not P&G or Amazon. P&G has a DRIP program but not a Roth IRA option.

The Roth IRA advantage:

As of 2014, the most that you can contribute to an IRA (Individual Retirement Account) is $5500 annually.

IRAs are tax-advantaged accounts in that they are given preferential tax treatment by the U.S. government to encourage people to save for retirement. For example, a regular account is subject to annual taxation for all capital gains and dividends that are realized, which means converted to cash. Dividends are issued in cash and are therefore taxable in the year they are issued. In some cases, dividends are stock dividends and those are not subject to tax until they are sold. Unrealized gains (paper gains) or stock price appreciation of unsold stock is not taxable. These gains will be realized when the stock is sold, which may not be for many years.

In a Traditional IRA account, stock may be sold and gains realized, but the money is only taxed when it is withdrawn from the account (distributed). And distribution may not occur for fifty years or more. Also, in a Traditional IRA account the money going in (contribution) is not taxed. The contribution is taxed, along with all dividends and gains, when it is taken as a distribution in retirement. This is called "tax-deferred" and favored by many people because their money grows faster and perhaps farther without the burden of initial taxation and interim taxation.

A Roth IRA is different from a Traditional IRA in that the contribution is taxed, but all gains and dividends from the contributions are not taxed at all, ever. There are critics who prefer the Traditional IRA; they point out that the additional contribution from the avoided tax produces enough gains and dividends to offset any advantage the Roth IRA has. This seems like a correct view but because the Roth IRA avoids taxation altogether, all accounting goes away.

With a Roth IRA you never have to worry about accounting and reporting gains which you do in a Traditional IRA, and in a Traditional IRA you have the additional burden of having to liquidate your entire account at some point. With a Roth IRA, there are no rules to worry about and when you get old one thing you don't need are tax rules – you are too old for that.

So building a large position in a Roth IRA is a very good idea. Since you are likely to do it from earned income that you have saved, which has already been taxed, there is no point in preferring a taxable account where not only will gains and dividends be taxed, but you will be faced with the tax accounting and reporting problem. With a Roth IRA, all that goes away. However, you are limited to $5500 per year. Still, over a 24-year period, the $5500 will have doubled three times to $44,000, which means the gains and dividends of $38,500 are entirely without tax liability or any accounting. And if you contribute $5500 per year for many years you will never have to worry about funding a retirement or about tax consequences in the retirement.

A Traditional and Roth IRA also have several other characteristics worth noting. IRA money is tax-advantaged only to encourage saving for old age; accordingly, the federal government has tax laws in place to discourage raiding retirement savings. For example, funds cannot be withdrawn from an IRA before age 59½ without penalty, presently a 10% penalty. But there are exceptions; some of the exceptions are for medical expenses, college expenses and a first home purchase. So this makes an IRA a good college funding vehicle.

Roth IRA for College Funding

Contributions into IRAs can only be made from earned income, meaning you must have a job to open an IRA account. But someday you may have children and be faced with the need to start a college fund for them. Once they start working, and this can be as early as age 8, for example, cutting lawns, you can get Social Security accounts for your children, actually they get them themselves, then hire your own children to cut the grass, pay them very handsomely, and put it into an IRA for them.

There are labor laws and government tax rules that must be negotiated, but if done with reasonableness it should work. The IRS may, for example, take issue with paying an 8-year old $1,000 to cut the grass. But the basic concept is perhaps the best college funding program there is.

Other college funding programs are complicated by issues like what if the child doesn't attend college, what happens to the money? And in such a case, who owns the money – the child for whom it was intended, or the adults who made the contributions? All this goes away in a child Roth IRA: the kid owns the money and can do anything he or she wants with it, without penalty, if the rules for withdrawals are followed.

And if the kid wants to go to college, the money is there for that. Remember, the core idea is not to get distracted by the minutiae of investment like Roth IRA rules or diversification controversy – the fact is that most people fail not because they don't follow IRA rules or they are poorly diversified, but because they have no investment program at all. Investment in the stock market is not for rich people, it is for poor people.

So to sum up: pick four stocks that are diversified by cyclicality, that are diversified globally and that are diversified internally. Try to pick stocks that offer a Roth IRA in a DRIP program. Accumulate $5500 in a taxable DRIP and then convert it to a Roth IRA. Continue contributing 5% of your income to the four Roth IRA DRIPS until you reach retirement age. As you see retirement coming, begin diversifying out into dividend-paying stocks and in retirement, draw-down at a rate not to exceed 7%, relying mostly on dividends.

Shown below are twelve stocks that offer direct investment in Roth IRAs. This list may be out of date, and it is always a good idea to research this out at DRIP plan administrators like Computershare. Remember, there is a $45 annual fee to custody a Roth IRA.

- Altria (*NYSE: MO*) Roth IRA – non-cyclical
- American Electric Power (*NYSE: AEP*) Roth IRA – non-cyclical
- Aqua America (*NYSE: WTR*) Roth IRA – non-cyclical
- AT&T (*NYSE: T*) Roth IRA – non-cyclical
- Campbell Soup (*NYSE: CPB*) Roth IRA – non-cyclical
- ExxonMobil (*NYSE: XOM*) Roth IRA – semi-cyclical
- Fannie Mae (*NYSE: FNM*) - cyclical
- Ford Motor (*NYSE: F*) Roth IRA - cyclical
- McDonald's (*NYSE: MCD*) Roth IRA – counter-cyclical
- Philip Morris (NYSE: PM) Roth IRA – non-cyclical
- Verizon (*NYSE: VZ*) Roth IRA – non-cyclical
- Wal-Mart Stores (*NYSE: WMT*) Roth IRA – counter-cyclical

The population of attractive stocks listed thus far are all you need to build an estate, and remember, a four-stock portfolio of strong, well-diversified companies further diversified by DCA investment is all the diversification you need. As we said earlier, you should know in what companies you are invested and why. In other words, invest in not only what you know, but what you like. But what you know and like will miss the industrial sector that has a number of quite remarkable companies that, like Exxon-Mobil, P&G, McDonald's and Amazon, have distinguished themselves by dominating the markets they serve, and you may wish to know about these companies.

On the following pages are listed public companies, some that you already know and that may be good investment candidates. They are listed here to help you think about companies you would like to invest in because they are leaders in their markets.

- Tiffany (TIF) Since 1837 Tiffany has been the #1 destination for wedding gifts and heirloom gifts for all occasions. Mostly cyclical, but people get married even in bad times. Dividend 1.60%.

- Harley-Davidson (HOG) has been not everyone's cup of tea since 1903, but they keep churning hogs out, and people of all stripes keep buying them. I once rode a Jap bike which was faster than most hogs, but I still got no respect. Definitely a cyclical play. Dividend 1.00%

- Kimberly-Clark (KMB) launched Kleenex in 1924 and has been a paper innovator ever since. A non-cyclical of the first order, or maybe even a counter-cyclical as people reach for a Kleenex to mop up their tears when times are bad. Dividend 4.30%.

- Intel (INTC) was co-founded by Robert Noyce, who in 1957 introduced a campus-like atmosphere to technology development and manufacturing that allowed his employees to achieve their maximum potential. Dividend 3.60%.

- Avon (AVP) has been calling since 1886 and does it worldwide. Dividend 3.40%.

- Caterpillar (CAT) Since 1925 Caterpillar has been the most prestigious name in heavy equipment for construction worldwide. A cyclical for sure. Dividend 1.60%.

- John Deere (DE) Since 1837 nothing has run quite like a Deere in agriculture and forestry worldwide. Dividend 1.50%.

- Colgate-Palmolive (CL) has been winning the toothpaste wars since 1896. Dividend 3.00%.

- HJ Heinz (HNZ) has been the #1 in fixin's for hot dogs and hamburgers since 1869. Also 56 other varieties and big in pickles, very big. Dividend 3.70%.

- General Electric (GE) has been on Charles Dow's industrial list since 1896. No other company quite like it: with its own derivative BCG (Boston Consulting Group) matrix of business mapping, GE continually re-invents itself. Dividend 2.90%.

- Southern Company (SO) Of all the utilities I called on nationally as a sales engineer, this was a standout for corporate culture devoted to excellence. Dividend 4.70%.

- DuPont (DD) Since 1802 DuPont has been committed to research for new products, establishing the first research laboratories in the U.S. Dividend 3.10%.

- Jardine Matheson (JMHLY.PK) Began in 1832 sending tea to England. Based in Hong Kong and experts in the China trade. If you want to hitch your wagon to the China star, this is the way to do it. No dividend.

- PACCAR Inc. (PCAR) Since 1939, PACCAR has been choosing to build the best trucks and not the most trucks – by paying attention to what drivers wanted. Today it is the dream of most truckers to own a Peterbilt. Dividend 1.00%.

- Kellogg Company (K) The older brother John employed his younger, good-for-nothing brother Will to make corn meal to be served to his patients at his sanatorium. One day Will forgot to package the drying meal and it dried out into, well, corn flakes. Will instantly saw the possibilities while his older brother couldn't get over his consternation at Will's ineptitude. They parted ways and Will went into the corn flake business. The rest is history. They are even eating Corn

Flakes in India now. Right up to his death, John never acknowledged Will's success. Kellogg's, the world's leading producer of cereal. Dividend 3.00%.

- Cummins Inc. (CMI) Since 1919 Cummins has been committed to perfecting the diesel engine. In 1940, Cummins offered the industry's first 100,000-mile warranty, and it has been on top ever since. Dividend 1.00%.

- Anheuser-Busch InBev (BUD) There is no question that Anheuser-Busch gained supremacy in the U.S. market for beer, making them a successful takeover target by InBev, a Belgian brewing powerhouse since 1366. InBev has also bought up the world's most renowned beer brands, including one of my favorites, Lowenbrau. My backup is Stella for Stella Artois. Dividend 0.70%.

- Parker Hannifin (PH) Since 1935 Parker Hannifin has sought to become the world's supplier of hydraulic systems to the transportation industry, making 58 acquisitions along the way. To those "in the know," like Charles Lindbergh, only Parker Hannifin will do. Dividend 1.40%.

- Unilever (UL) Beginning in the 1890s, Unilever became the soap maker and grocer to the world – somewhat the English equivalent of Procter&Gamble but with a food dimension. Unilever owns Lipton, which is globally the most recognized name in tea, even in China. Dividend 3.90%.

- 3M Co. (MMM) Like Intel, 3M Company has since 1902 grown by empowering its workers to innovate. This organic, ground-up process has propelled 3M into leadership positions in multiple business sectors with products such as Scotch Tape® and Post-it Notes®. This company is perhaps the most diversified company in the world, and like DuPont, has innovation in the gene pool. Dividend 2.40%.

- Schlumberger (SLB) A French company that is as dominant in global oil-field services as McDonald's is in fast-food.

- Boeing Co. (BA) The end of WWI saw the aviation market flooded with surplus airplanes, and while their competitors went out of business, Boeing began making furniture. Since then, Boeing has been an innovation leader, eventually, for a time, becoming the world's only global airliner builder. That ended with the rise of EADS, a French-British consortium, but Boeing keeps making the right decisions, like staying away from the supersonic detour eventually realized and then dropped by EADS. Dividend 2.30%.

- Michelin (ML.PA) Michelin has led tire innovation since 1888, including the radial tire (1946), eventually becoming the world's largest tire manufacturer. Michelin came to my attention in graduate business school, when I was studying for a case discussion on the company. I learned that when a boiler had to be replaced at one of their factories, they constructed a tunnel into the factory to prevent spies from infiltrating the plant for trade secrets. This certainly illustrated a company that both produced and protected value. The publication of the Michelin guide is a bonus. Traveling in Italy, my wife and I came upon a hidden gem of a restaurant that was off the beaten path, but in the Michelin guide.

- Clorox Corp. (CLX) From 1913 up until the buyout by Procter & Gamble in 1957, Clorox concentrated on making Clorox brand bleach the undisputed quality leader. In 1969, P&G was forced by the FTC to divest Clorox, which then went on a hunt to remake itself into a P&G lite. This failed but left Clorox with some decent brands, like Glad bags and Kingsford charcoal. Still, this is an interesting investment not so much for the management as for the unshakeable position of Clorox, perhaps won during WWII, when the company's management decided to sell less but full-strength product in response to wartime conservation policies, thus establishing it as the quality leader. No matter how bad the management, they can't seem to shake that Clorox brand. Dividend 3.20%.

- Nestle (NESN.VX) Nestle is a result of a fierce American-Swiss rivalry for condensed milk, baby food, and the use of condensed milk to make chocolate bars. Finally, in 1905 the companies merged and today have no direct competitors for a wide assortment of global brands and markets, all connected to food. No dividend.

- Eaton Corp. (ETN) Since 1916, Eaton has been an aggressive global aggregator of businesses that contribute to process management; important products are axles, valves and industrial controls. You don't hear too much about Eaton because they are too busy doing good. Dividend 2.60%.

- United Parcel Service (UPS) Started in 1907, UPS adopted its familiar "Pullman" brown color in 1930 because of communicating a quality of "neat, dignified and professional." Today the company continues that tradition, but has integrated backwards toward the shipper end by offering services that expedite shipment and delivery. For example, the lobster that arrives at your door from Maine most likely was routed through the UPS lobster pound in Louisville. Lobster in, lobster out. Dividend 2.80%.

- American Express (AXP) The 22nd most valuable brand and one of the top 30 most admired companies in the world. This puts Amex well ahead of their competition. In addition, Amex cards have the largest market share of U.S. credit card transactions. But while I have been a devoted user since 1975, I became a believer when I used an American Express traveler's check on a European train to pay a fare and got too much change back. When I objected, the conductor stated that American Express traveler's checks were better than cash, receiving a better rate of exchange. Dividend 1.60%.

- Microsoft (MSFT) Bill Gates, while perhaps not overtly demonstrating any personal excellence, seems to have put together a company of enduring excellence. They make mistakes, but seem to have an ability to recover and they have successfully negotiated competition from the free generic rival, Linux. Microsoft is a company the world cannot do without. Dividend 2.50%.

- Southwest Airlines (LUV) Southwest was created in 1967, reportedly on the back of a cocktail napkin. Herb Kelleher and Rollin King set out to establish a new aviation culture and model. Frightened by this attack on their turf, the big airlines fought back, keeping Southwest on the ground, for a time. Today Southwest is the nation's largest airline. What impressed me most, however, was when I read that at the height of one of the cyclical run-ups in petroleum prices, Southwest had purchased forwards on cheap fuel, a huge amount, keeping them flying through the crisis. Kelleher died but the airline seems to have retained his spirit. Dividend 0.50%.

- Volkswagen (VLKAY) Over-the-Counter ADR for this German company that has been producing the people's car since 1937. VW is the second largest carmaker in the world and has three cars in the top ten bestsellers of all time.

- Santander (SAN) A Spanish company. From their website: *"Founded in 1857, the Santander Group is one of the largest banks in the world with 102 million customers, 14,500 branches and 190,000 employees. As a leading bank in the United Kingdom, Latin America and Europe, Santander is geographically and financially diversified. We were recognized in 2012 as Best Global Bank by Euromoney, ranked as a top Greenest Global Bank in 2013 by Bloomberg BusinessWeek and named 2013 Sustainable Global Bank of the Year - Transactions by the Financial Times."*

- Atlas-Copco (ATLCY) Basic construction tools since 1873 and now in 180 countries. This is an internally well-diversified company with a stellar reputation for quality. Being a Swedish company, it is a nice way to diversify a portfolio geographically. Yield 3%.

What other companies can you think of? Stumped? Point your browser to www.interbrand.com and you will see what the leading global, mostly consumer brands are. But the great industrial brands do eventually become household words, like Caterpillar, IBM, Arcelor-Mittal, Alcoa, PPG and others. All are companies that, together with the ones listed, consumer and industrial, through a long evolutionary history have become iconic companies that have grown a global following of devoted customers who seek out their brand and will even pay a handsome premium to get it.

These are the companies you want – stable, strong, innovative and profitable. A much better value than a company like GM that is coasting and a much better value than any mutual fund that sacrifices profit for the confusion of numbers and the illusion of "safety."

Chapter 11

Taxes

IN ECONOMIC SPEAK, *externalities* are things that cannot be allocated to any discrete buyers, like the services you use to get to school every day. What about the street you use to get to school on, or the school bus that takes you to school? If the city charged people to use the roads and charged students to ride the school bus, the cost of collection would be a big burden. Can you imagine toll-takers on every city street or meters in cars to be read monthly by meter readers? Or how about school bus drivers collecting fares? What a burden that would be. And then there would be some students who would walk to school or get driven by their parents, creating a traffic jam at the school. All of this goes away by the mechanism of taxes levied on homeowners for city-supplied services like streets and school bus service.

The externality term refers to the idea that although all homeowners will pay taxes, not all homeowners drive or have children. For them, that portion of the city tax they pay but don't demand services for is an *externality* – something that cannot be helped.

The classic explanation of externality is a coal-fired power plant that deposits coal dust on neighborhood laundry that has just been hung up to dry on outside clotheslines. There is a cost to this, and it will be borne by the homeowner and not the power plant. Externalities are things that are difficult to charge for and so the costs are misallocated: school tax for people without children and the cost of ruined laundry borne by the homeowner.

There are many externalities beyond these two. There is the cost of national defense where not all citizens would pay for all defense initiatives, but they don't have a choice as long as they are required to pay taxes. Highways connecting cities and states are paid for through taxes although not all taxpayers use them. State colleges are paid for by state taxes. Garbage collection is free in many cities, along with policing and fire departments, all included in city taxation. So taxation is a requirement and turns out to be the most efficient way to pay for public services that cannot easily be allocated to discrete users only. In short, taxes are a fact of life: city taxes, state taxes, national taxes.

Types of taxes

In addition to the different taxing authorities, there are different taxes. There are excise taxes that are taxes levied on goods people buy, like gasoline. When excise taxes are levied on tobacco and liquor, they are called "sin" taxes and usually shift a disproportionate burden of public cost to that subset of the population that chooses to use tobacco and liquor.

Sales tax is levied on everyday products like items from a store; sales taxes are considered "regressive" taxes in that all people, rich and poor, pay the same rate of tax. Because these taxes are regressive, some items are not taxed, like necessities such as food and clothing in many states.

Another necessity that is taxed is home ownership. Renters do not pay tax directly but will see their rents rise to help the landlord pay the tax on the property he is renting out. Homeowners pay real estate tax directly; it too is a regressive tax in that rich and poor pay the same rate. But rich people wind up paying more tax because they live in more expensive homes that carry higher taxes.

Income tax is a national tax collected by the U.S. Internal Revenue Service and is sometimes referred to as a "progressive" tax because the tax rate rises with income, whereby a rich person might pay an income tax rate of say 35%, while a poor person might only pay a tax rate of 20% and in some cases a lower rate or no tax at all.

Income taxes are also levied by states, and in some cases cities as well. Income taxes are the workhorses of the tax world and provide most of the revenue needed to provide the many public services the public demands. It may amaze you to learn that income taxes are a fairly recent phenomenon and throughout history have been pretty unpopular. During our country's early years there was no income tax and government was paid for by import tax. All those imports the public demanded, like tea and sugar and other spices, were taxed upon importation; those taxes then paid for government.

Government vs. Business

A country's population may be generally divided into two groups: public employees and private employees, or employees of businesses. A major difference between the two groups is that while both need to have salaries increased periodically to account for inflation, the limit of public employee wage increases is the amount that can be taxed, theoretically. Private employee wage growth is limited by the amount of revenue and profit a business realizes from its operations. If there is a decline in business or profitability, the private enterprise will cut back on expenses and the number of workers to bring wage expense back in line with revenue and profit. In the public sector, tax collection will be proportional to the business cycle as well, but the termination of public-sector workers is unheard of. So unlike a private business that inflates and deflates with the economy, the public sector only inflates.

It should come as no surprise that with the inability to deflate during business-cycle downturns, public taxation must ramp up to cover the shortfall. But there is a limit to how much tax the public will pay; the public disorder that too high a tax will prompt is well remembered by taxing authorities. In fact, the revolution that brought our country into existence as a separate entity from Great Britain was an issue over taxation. So the taxing authorities are keenly aware of the limits on taxing. However, they have found a work-around – borrowing. Taxing authorities issue bonds to cover costs they can't tax for and then issue more bonds to pay for the bonds they issued earlier.

Where the Money Comes From

Most business start-ups fail because of a poor understanding of how the business thesis will translate into revenue and profit. But even some of the most attractive ideas and well-thought-out business strategies fail because some factor was not sufficiently considered or considered at all. The classic tale of this hazard is the Ford Motor Company story of the Edsel automobile. Ford management thought that the nation was ready for a car that was a little more deluxe than a Ford but not quite in the luxury level with Mercury – a car in-between was needed. They brought out the Edsel, and it was a huge flop. Soon after, the Edsel program was cancelled. In this case, the buying public, the market, was the disciplinarian. The market decides what is and is not needed and the market decided the Edsel was not needed, so the Edsel program was cancelled.

There are inevitably "Edsels" in the public domain, like the Iraq war engaged in by the George W. Bush administration that cost well over $100 billion. It is generally accepted now that the Iraq War was an error, but that in no way mitigates the cost of the war and the tax burden it imposes, not to mention the borrowing it prompted. But because the public did not directly pay for the war it went on anyway. This is the difference between business and government – in business, whatever doesn't work gets cancelled; in government, whatever doesn't work is paid for by borrowing.

Eventually that borrowing shows up as increased taxes and reduced services. So it can pretty well be taken as a certainty: taxes are going up.

Tax Policy

Long before out-of-control taxation prompts a public outcry, the taxing authorities will take note of the uneven effect taxes have on the economy. For example, sin taxes can be quite high without disrupting the supply of tobacco and liquor and the economy that those activities produce. The last thing anybody wants is the loss of the tobacco and liquor economies: smokers and drinkers would suffer immeasurably but so would the government which depends upon the revenue tobacco and liquor taxes produce. In consequence of this, taxes are very finely tuned to extract the maximum revenue without disrupting the underlying economy.

Such fine tuning leads to a tax code that covers a gazillion different sources of revenue and how they are to be taxed with minimum disruption to their underlying economies, which prompts a very complicated tax reporting program that allows deductions for a large variety of expenses. This has spawned a large and national business in tax preparation. It takes professionals devoted to tax preparation to understand and take advantage of all the deductions.

One reason for all the deductions is to satisfy all the parties. As soon as one group gets a tax break, complaining breaks out, which is ultimately tamped down by a new deduction for the complaining group. So everybody gets a tax break of one sort or another, so everybody feels like they are getting a break; this brings about a level of dissatisfaction that keeps the grumbling down to a manageable level.

Avoiding vs Evading Tax

Avoiding tax is legal; evading tax is not. Annually, every wage earner in America is required to file an income tax return that documents income and expenses to calculate taxable income and the resulting tax bill for the year. Using every single arcane tax policy to minimize tax is legal and distinguishes avoidance from evasion. Not reporting income is evasion and is illegal.

Tax-Deferred Retirement Accounts

Since tax has the effect of putting a brake on the economy, Congress has taken the tax off of retirement savings to spur people to save for their later years when they may not be able to work or work as hard anymore. Without retirement savings citizens might have to depend upon the state for care; to head off this potential raid on the public treasury Congress has developed various tax loopholes to incentivize people to save for retirement.

The tax is not actually removed from retirement savings, only postponed. And for a society avidly kicking the can down the road on any unpleasantness, like a tax bill, it works. Here is how it works. Say you work at a job that pays you $100 a week. Every Monday, you get a paycheck for the previous week, but the check is for only $70. What happened to that $100 you earned? Well, there were deductions for Social Security, which is the government-sponsored retirement program, and then perhaps $20 was taken out for income tax and a few dollars for various other deductions. The $20 tax withholding is for an anticipated income-tax rate of 20% on $100. Now say you decided to contribute $10 to a retirement account. Then you would only be taxed on $90 for an income-tax withholding of $18 instead of $20. So you saved $2 in tax and put away $10 for retirement. The actual cost to you for the $10 retirement contribution is only $8.

This sounds like an incredible deal until you learn that you can't touch that money until you are 59½ years old, and then only after paying the deferred income tax on it. Plus the tax rate will be the highest tax rate there is – Ordinary Income Tax rate or the default rate you pay after taking all of the tax loopholes you are entitled to. This may sound like a totally bad deal, but the theory is that during your earning years you will be at your highest tax bracket and during your retirement years you will be at your lowest tax bracket. If you defer paying 20% tax and later pay only a 15% tax on the same money, you have saved 5%.

Roth IRA accounts

As described earlier, if you are not too impressed with the above formula a Roth IRA account might be good for you. In a Roth you put aside retirement money but only after it has been taxed, so only about 80% of the Traditional IRA contribution. Then, again at age 59½, you may begin to take withdrawals, but since the seed money has already been taxed there is no tax on withdrawals. This may sound like it is not that big of a deal, but if you invest money over say a 40-year or 50-year period, the total accumulation will be mostly dividends and gains on investment rather than the original taxed contributions, and since these gains are "Rotherized," they are not taxed at all. The naysayers to this idea argue that by losing the 20% tax deferral on the original contributions, the loss of income from the lost deferral is equal to the gain on the avoided tax. This may be true but the counterargument is that tax rates have nowhere to go but up and paying a smaller tax now beats paying a larger tax later. However, a Roth IRA has four other characteristics that offer significant advantage:

1. Forgetfulness. As with other unpleasantness in life, unpleasant details tend to be forgotten, so it may come as a nasty end-of-the-year surprise that those Traditional IRA withdrawals taken over the past years now require a tax to be paid. A no-tax Roth avoids this unpleasant surprise.

2. Uncle Sam wants to tax your money but if you don't withdraw it, it can't be taxed. This has been thought of by the taxing authorities. There is a 50% penalty on that portion of the withdrawal that has not met Required Minimum Distributions (RMD) thresholds. With a Roth, there are no RMDs.

3. Contributions into Traditional IRAs must end at age 70½. For a Roth IRA, there is no age limit on contributions.

4. No tax on Roth withdrawals means no tax reporting. In a non-retirement account, the original cost of a stock purchase, the "cost-basis," must be documented so that you can calculate the capital gain when you sell. This can be very challenging, particularly for multiple shares purchased over many years. In a Traditional IRA, cost-basis is irrelevant because all the money withdrawn is taxed at the same rate so it doesn't matter whether it is capital gain, dividend or contribution. In a Roth, dividends and capital gains are not taxed, so no cost-basis recordkeeping, no tax and no tax reporting.

But, whether you choose a Traditional IRA or a Roth IRA, it is still better than a non-retirement account where contributions are taxed and dividends and capital gains are taxed annually, all adding to your annual tax bill and the accompanying record-keeping.

When stock holdings appreciate there is an "unrealized" capital gain that is not subject to tax, but if the holding is sold at a profit, the gain is "realized" and taxed. Cash dividends are also subject to tax as distributed, but stock dividends are not taxed unless sold and converted to cash. Dividends and capital gains, even realized capital gains, inside of retirement accounts are not taxed until withdrawn as a cash "distribution."

Loss Carry-forwards

It probably won't make much difference whether you use a Traditional or Roth account to save for retirement. What will eventually count is whether you saved and invested at all. But there is one area of tax policy that is crucial to investment and that is the concept of "Loss Carry-forwards."

Loss carry-forwards are losses that can be used to offset tax. Here is how they work. Since retirement accounts have tax advantages they are treated differently, which includes the requirement that they not be withdrawn prior to age 59½. After reaching age 59½ a withdrawal may be taken, which is termed a "distribution." The word *distribution* is used because the funds are inaccessible to the owner until action is taken to withdraw them. If funds are withdrawn prior to reaching age 59½ there is a 10% federal penalty, so in addition to paying tax on the distribution the U.S. government takes 10%. This is to encourage saving for retirement which, as we have discussed, keeps elderly people off the welfare rolls and financing themselves.

Both taxable and tax-deferred accounts will, over time, have a history of rises and falls, both unrealized and realized, as when a holding is sold or liquidated. In a retirement account, the only figure that matters is the final figure because gains inside the account are not taxed even when gains are realized. For retirement accounts, there is no tax issue until withdrawal. But in taxable accounts, all dividends and realized gains are taxed in the year they are booked and "realized." Consequently, over a period of years, each account will have a history of gains, losses and taxes.

Taxes are only due on gains, so if an account in previous years has accumulated losses, then those losses can be used to offset tax in profitable years. The tax liability does not kick in until the account has been profitable as a whole. It is best to illustrate this concept with an example:

	Cash-in	Gains	Losses	Loss Carry-forwards	Ending Value	Tax Liability on Gains
Taxable Account	$10,000	$15,000	$5,000	$5,000	$20,000	$5,000
Traditional IRA Account	$10,000	$15,000	$5,000	$0	$20,000	$10,000

In the above example the cash flows are identical, $10,000 in gains and $5,000 in accumulated losses, but the losses have no value in a non-taxable account, while in a taxable account losses may be used to offset gains for the purpose of reducing tax exposure. But unlike the above illustration, tax-loss carry-forwards are "harvested" every year at tax time, not at some future date. So the above illustration is to portray the concept rather than the practice of harvesting loss carry-forwards.

The purpose of this book is to show you that trading in and out of volatile stocks is a losing game, and as soon as you do that, pointing to the long-term rise in value of the stock market has no meaning because the long-term S&P 500 results are only for those who get in and stay in. If you don't do that, then your chart is whatever you make it. For most people it is a chart of losses over time.

Remember, when somebody cites the long run return on the S&P 500, for example, the return cited is only for a fixed investment clocked between two points. Most people don't realize that. But DCA investors do even better than reported long run returns, because they are biasing their investment toward cheaper shares.

There are three sources of leaks in investment accounts:

1. Taxes.
2. Market losses.
3. Transaction costs.

You can reduce tax with an IRA or 401(k) retirement account. You can eliminate market losses by getting in and staying in and using DCA. And transaction costs, a potentially large drag on DCA investing, can be reduced by using DRIPs and ShareBuilder.

AFTERWORD

A NUMBER OF YEARS AGO I was privileged to have watched a presentation at the University of Nebraska, where Warren Buffett and Bill Gates, perhaps two of the world's wealthiest men at the time, or in any case, very, very wealthy men, were seated on a stage in an event that invited students to ask the two men any questions that were on their mind. One student did a very wise thing and asked an open-ended question, not a closed-end question that can be answered with a "yes" or a "no." The question was: *"What advice do you have for someone just graduating from college?"*

Bill Gates went first and very predictably went off on a riff about college graduates having the opportunity to go into the IT field, and then he gave some detail on possible IT choices, software, etc. Then it was Warren's turn. The "Sage of Omaha," as he is sometimes referred to, challenged the students to do the following: *"Make a list of the ten people you admire most,"* he said. *"Then make a list of the ten people you admire the least. When you are finished, study the two lists and consider the differences in characteristics between the two groups and you will begin to understand who you are."*

The reason I mention it here is to make the point that investment cannot be separated from the individual. People bring their entire life-experience to bear on all decisions, particularly investment decisions. The purpose of this book is to help you take control of your financial life, and that will only come about if you take control of your personal life. Following Buffett's advice will help put you on the road to taking ownership of your life, and that will be a crucial step along the way in taking control of your financial life.

A Final Word

Since the founding of the American republic, there has been a gradual, sometimes bumpy, but inexorable aggregation of wealth and power and more wealth and more power by an American elite that has resulted in an American landscape that today is largely fixed, and no longer reflects the "Land of Opportunity" that created the republic in the first place. Politics, education, careers, jobs and wages are increasingly being driven to support an agenda of control by a power/wealth elite. Just since the 1950s, when I was a youth, the change has been both dramatic and palpable.

The stock market is one of the few areas of American life that still functions on a level playing field. And I don't mean Wall Street. I am speaking about the American market for stocks founded in New York in 1792 under a Buttonwood tree. That stock market.

The power elite have no advantage in the stock market; it is totally random. Therefore, the stock market is one of the very few venues you will have to create the wealth you need to educate your children and provide for your own declining years. It is there for you. Use it!

www.ingramcontent.com/pod-product-compliance
Lightning Source LLC
Chambersburg PA
CBHW060019210326
41520CB00009B/936